This volume is one of a series of short biographies derived from *The New Grove Dictionary of Music and Musicians, second edition* (London, 2001). The four volumes that inaugurate this series were chosen by John Tyrrell as outstanding examples of the biographical articles in the new edition; they are printed here with little alteration.

Laura Macy
London, 2001

THE NEW GROVE®

WAGNER

Barry Millington

GROVE

MACMILLAN PUBLISHERS LIMITED, LONDON

PALGRAVE, NEW YORK, NY

© Macmillan Publishers Limited, 2002

First published in
The New Grove Dictionary of Music and Musicians®, second edition
edited by Stanley Sadie, 2001

The New Grove and *The New Grove Dictionary of Music and Musicians*
are registered trademarks of Macmillan Publishers Limited, London,
and its associated companies

First published in the UK 2002 by Macmillan Publishers Limited, London

This edition is distributed within the UK and Europe
by Macmillan Publishers Limited, London.

First published in North America in 2002 by Palgrave,
175 Fifth Avenue, New York, NY

Palgrave is the new global publishing imprint of St. Martin's Press LLC Scholarly and
Reference Division and Palgrave Publishers Ltd. (formerly Macmillan Press Ltd.)

British Library Cataloguing in Publication Data
The New Grove Wagner (The New Grove composer biographies series)
  1. Wagner, Richard, 1813–1883 2. Composers – Germany – Biography
  I. Sadie, Stanley, 1930– II. Tyrrell, John
  780.9'2

  ISBN 0-333-80410-4

Library of Congress Cataloguing-in Publication Data
The New Grove Wagner : the New Grove composer biographies / edited by
Barry Millington
    p. cm. - (Grove music)
  Includes biographical references and index
  ISBN 0-312-23324-8 (pbk.)
  1. Wagner, Richard, 1813–1883. 2. Composers–Germany–Biography.
  I. Title: New Grove composer biographies. II. Millington, Barry.
  III. Series.
  ML410.W1 N46 2000
  782.1'092–dc21
  [B]   00-031121

Contents

Abbreviations

General

A – alto
acc. – accompaniment, accompanied by
arr(s) – arrangement(s), arranged by/for
attrib(s). – attribution(s), attributed to; ascription(s), ascribed to
Aug – August
aut. – autumn
b – born
B – bass [voice]
Bar – baritone
chap. – chapter
comp(s). – composer(s), composed (by)
cond(s). – conductor(s), conducted by
CT – Connecticut
d - died
Dec – December
DG – Deutsche Grammophon
diss. – dissertation
ed(s). – editor(s), edited (by)
edn(s) – edition(s)
Eng. – English
ENO – English National Opera
facs. – facsimile(s)
Feb – February
fl – flute
Fr. – French
frag(s). – fragment(s)
Ger. – German
inc. – incomplete
incl. – includes, including
Jan – January
Jb – Jahrbuch

Jg – Jahrgang [year of publication/volume]
Kgl – Königlich(e, er, es) [Royal]
LA – Louisiana
lib(s) – libretto(s)
Mar – March
MD – Maryland
movt(s). – movement(s)
MS(S) – manuscript(s)
NE- Nebraska
NJ – New Jersey
NY – New York
no(s). – number(s)
nr – near
Oct – October
op(p). – opus, opera (plural of opus)
orch – orchestra(tion), orchestral
orchd – orchestrated (by)
orig. – original(ly)
ov. – overture
p(p). – page(s)
PA – Philadelphia
perf(s). – performance(s), performed (by)
pf – piano [instrument]
prol(s). – prologue(s)
ps –piano score
pt – part
pubd – published
qt - quartet
R – photographic reprint [edn of score or early printed source]

reorchd – reorchestrated (by)
repr. – reprinted
rev(s). – revision(s); revised (by/for)
S – soprano
Sept – September
ser. – series
spr. – spring
St – Saint
str – string(s)
sum. – summer
suppl(s). – supplement(s), supplementary
sym(s). – symphony, symphonies, symphonic
T – tenor
trans. – translation, translated (by)
transc(s). – transcription(s), transcribed by/for
U. – University
unacc. – unaccompanied
unpubd – unpublished
v – voice
vol(s). – volume(s)
vs – vocal score
vn – violin
vv – voices
WI – Wisconsin
wint. – winter

Bibliographic

19CM – 19th Century Music
AnMc – Analecta musicologica
AMw – Archiv für Musikwissenschaft
AMz – Allgemeine (deutsche) Musik-Zeitung/Musikzeitung (1874-1943)
COJ – Cambridge Opera Journal
GfMKB – Gesellschaft fur Musikforschung: Kongress-Bericht [1950-]
IMSCR – International Musicological Society: Congress Report [1930-]
IRMAS – International Review of Music Aesthetics and Sociology

JAMS – Journal of the American Musicological Society
JbSIM - Jahrbuch des Staatlichen Instituts für Musikforschung Preussischer Kulturbesitz
JM – Journal of Musicology
MAn – Music Analysis
Mf – Die Musikforschung
ML – Music & Letters
MQ – Musical Quarterly
MR – Music Review
MT – Musical Times

NOHM – The New Oxford History of Music (Oxford, 1954–90)
NZM – Neue Zeitschrift für Musik
ÖMz – Österreichische Musikzeitschrift
OQ – Opera Quarterly
PRMA – Proceedings of the Royal Musical Association
ReM – Revue musicale

Library sigla

A-Wgm – Austria, Vienna, Gesellschaft der Musikfreunde

A-Wn – Austria, Vienna, Österreichische Nationalbibliothek, Musiksammlung

CH-W – Switzerland, Winterthur, Stadtbibliothek

D-Dl – Germany, Dresden, Sächsische Landesbibliothek – Staats- und Universitäts-Bibliothek, Musikabteilung

D-LEu – Germany, Leipzig, Karl-Marx-Universität, Universitätsbibliothek, Bibliotheca Albertina

D-Mbs – Germany, Munich, Bayerische Staatsbibliothek

D-Ngm – Germany, Nuremberg, Germanisches National-Museum, Bibliothek

F-Pn – France, Paris, Bibliothèque Nationale de France

F-Po – France, Paris, Bibliothèque-Musée de l'Opéra

GB-Lbl – Great Britain, London, British Library

H-Bo – Hungary, Budapest, Állami Operaház

S-Smf – Sweden, Stockholm, Stiftelsen Musikkulturens Främjande

US-NYp – USA, New York, Public Library at Lincoln Center, Music Division

US-NYpm – USA, New York, Pierpont Morgan Library

US-PHci – USA, Philadelphia, Curtis Institute of Music, Library

US-PRu – USA, Princeton (NJ), Princeton University, Firestone Memorial Library

US-STu – USA, Palo Alto (CA), Universtiy, Memorial Library of Music, Department of Special Collections of the Cecil H. Green Library

US-Wc – USA, Washington, DC, Library of Congress, Music Division

List of Illustrations

R ichard Wagner's contribution to the development of music was so far-reaching as to be almost incalculable. One of the key figures in the history of opera, he was largely responsible for altering its orientation in the 19th century. His programme of artistic reform, though not executed to the last detail, accelerated the trend towards organically conceived, through-composed structures, as well as influencing the development of the orchestra, of a new breed of singer, and of various aspects of theatrical practice.

---

1. FORMATIVE YEARS AND EARLY CAREER

THE FORMATIVE YEARS: 1813–32

It is both fitting and psychologically congruous that a question mark should hover over the identity of the father and mother of the composer whose works resonate so eloquently with themes of parental anxiety. Wilhelm Richard Wagner was born in Leipzig on 22 May 1813. His 'official' father was the police actuary Carl Friedrich Wagner, but the boy's adoptive father, the actor-painter Ludwig Geyer, who took responsibility for the child on Carl Friedrich's death in November 1813, may possibly have been the real father. Wagner himself was never sure, though any concern he may have had about Geyer's supposed Jewish origins would have been misplaced: Geyer was of incontrovertibly Protestant stock. Recent research has further established that Wagner's mother Johanna was not the illegitimate daughter of Prince Constantin of Saxe-Weimar-Eisenach, as previously believed, but his mistress (Gregor-Dellin, I 1985).

Wagner's formal education began on 2 December 1822 at the Kreuzschule in Dresden, where his mother and stepfather had moved to enable Geyer to undertake engagements for the Hoftheater. On returning to Leipzig with his mother and sisters Richard entered the Nicolaischule on 21 January 1828, but school studies were less enthusiastically pursued than theatrical and musical interests, which resulted in a 'vast tragic drama' called *Leubald* and conscientious perusal of a well-known composition treatise. Harmony lessons (initially in secret) with

1

a local musician, Christian Gottlieb Müller (1828–31), were followed by enrolment at Leipzig University (23 February 1831) to study music, and a short but intensive period of study with the Kantor of the Thomaskirche, Christian Theodor Weinlig (about six months from October 1831).

In his autobiographical writings Wagner later played down the significance of his musical education in order to cultivate the notion of the untutored genius. But its fruits were evident in a series of keyboard and orchestral works written by spring 1832 and particularly in the Beethovenian Symphony in C major which followed shortly after. A genuine passion for Beethoven, while confirmed by such works and the piano transcription of the Ninth Symphony made in 1830–31, was exaggerated in another typical piece of mythification: Wagner's account of a supposedly momentous portrayal of Leonore in *Fidelio* by the soprano Wilhelmine Schröder-Devrient in Leipzig in 1829 is undermined by the unavailability of any evidence that the singer gave such a performance. Yet the fable (probably a semi-conscious conflation of two separate events) attests to the young composer's ambition to be proclaimed the rightful heir to the symphonic tradition embodied in Beethoven.

Wagner's first attempt at an operatic project was a pastoral opera modelled on Goethe's *Die Laune des Verliebten* (? early 1830); the work was aborted with only a scene for three female voices and a tenor aria written. His second project, *Die Hochzeit*, was conceived in October–November 1832, while he was visiting the estate of Count Pachta at Pravonín, near Prague. Based on a story from J.G.G. Büsching's *Ritterzeit und Ritterwesen*, *Die Hochzeit* was a grisly tale of dark passions, treachery and murder. The libretto, according to Wagner's autobiography, *Mein Leben*, was destroyed by him as a demonstration of confidence in the judgment of his sister Rosalie. Such music as was completed, between December 1832 and February 1833 – an introduction, chorus and septet – survives.

EARLY CAREER: 1833–42

Wagner's first professional appointment, secured by his brother Albert, was as chorus master at the theatre in Würzburg. There he encountered repertory works by Marschner, Weber, Paer, Cherubini, Rossini and Auber, of which composers the first two influenced him most strongly in his musical setting of *Die Feen* (1833–4), a working by Wagner himself (he was to write all his own librettos) of Gozzi's *La donna serpente*. Returning to Leipzig at the beginning of 1834, he came into contact with the charismatic radical Heinrich Laube (a family friend) and other members of the progressive literary and political movement Junges Deutschland. The writers associated with this uncoordinated grouping, including Karl Gutzkow, Ludolf Wienbarg, Heinrich Heine and Ludwig Börne, rejected not only the Classicism of Goethe and Mozart but also what they regarded as the reactionary, socially irrelevant and sentimentally conceived Romanticism of Weber and E.T.A. Hoffmann. They turned instead for inspiration to Italy and to the French Utopian socialists, especially the Saint-Simonists, spurning Catholic mysticism and morality in favour of hedonism and sensuality. It was under these influences that Wagner wrote his essays *Die deutsche Oper* (1834) and *Bellini* (1837), celebrating the italianate capacity for bel canto expressiveness, and his next opera *Das Liebesverbot* (1835–6), relocating Shakespeare's *Measure for Measure* in a sun-soaked, pleasure-filled Mediterranean setting; the chief musical models adopted were, appropriately, Bellini and Auber.

It was carnal rather than aesthetic considerations, according to Wagner, that persuaded him to accept a post as musical director of the travelling theatre company run by Heinrich Bethmann: he had fallen instantly in love with one of the leading ladies, Christine Wilhelmine ('Minna') Planer. However, during his term with Bethmann's company (1834–6) he also gained valuable conducting experience and saw *Das Liebesverbot* onto the boards (29 March 1836) for what was to be the only performance in his lifetime.

Minna continued to pursue her theatrical career with engagements at the Königstädtisches Theater in Berlin and then in Königsberg. Negotiations for Wagner to secure the musical directorship of the opera in the latter town were protracted until 1 April 1837, but in the meantime he had sketched a prose scenario for a grand opera, *Die hohe Braut*, which he sent to Scribe in Paris in the hope that a libretto by him might inspire an Opéra commission. It was Wagner who eventually produced a libretto for *Die hohe Braut* (in Dresden in 1842); it was offered first to Karl Reissiger and then to Ferdinand Hiller, but was finally set by Jan Bedřich Kittl. An already tempestuous relationship with Minna was sealed by their marriage on 24 November 1836. Within months she had abandoned him in favour of a merchant called Dietrich; the rift had been healed only in part when Wagner took up a new post as musical director of the theatre in Riga, a Latvian town (part of the Russian Empire) colonized by Germans. He made the journey alone, arriving on 21 August 1837, but subsequently shared his cramped apartment not only with Minna, but also with her sister Amalie (who had taken up an appointment as singer at the theatre) and a wolf cub. Conditions at the small theatre were similarly constricted and the management unimaginative, though Wagner's enterprise and initiative did result in a series of subscription concerts.

In the summer of 1838 he turned his attention to a comic opera based on a tale from *The Thousand and One Nights*, calling it *Männerlist grösser als Frauenlist, oder Die glückliche Bärenfamilie*. He completed the libretto and began to set it in the manner of a Singspiel, but abandoned it in order to concentrate on a major project that had been simmering since he had read, the previous year, Edward Bulwer-Lytton's novel about the Roman demagogue Rienzi. The poem and some of the music of the five-act grand opera *Rienzi* had been written by August 1838. The Riga appointment turned out to be as precarious for Wagner as his marriage, and after a contractual wrangle he determined to try his luck in the home of grand opera, Paris.

The departure from Riga had to be clandestine; Wagner and his wife were heavily in debt and their passports had been impounded. Under cover of night, Wagner, Minna and their Newfoundland dog, Robber, clambered through a ditch marking the border, under the noses of armed Cossack guards. Then, reaching the Prussian port of Pillau (now Baltiysk), they were smuggled on board a small merchant vessel, the *Thetis*, bound for London. The dangerous, stormy crossing and the crew's shouts echoing round the granite walls of a Norwegian fjord were later represented by Wagner as the creative inspiration for *Der fliegende Holländer*. If any ideas for text or music were jotted down at the time of the sea crossing (July–August 1839), the evidence has not survived. Crossing the Channel from Gravesend to Boulogne, Wagner was received there by Meyerbeer, who listened to Wagner's reading of the libretto of *Rienzi* and promised to provide letters of introduction to Duponchel and Habeneck, respectively the director and conductor of the Paris Opéra.

Wagner spent a dismal, penurious two and a half years (September 1839 to April 1842) in Paris, a victim of the sharp social divisions of Louis-Philippe's July Monarchy which reserved wealth and privilege for a bourgeois élite. He was forced to earn his keep by making hack arrangements of operatic selections and by musical journalism in which he lambasted the mediocrities perpetrated by the Opéra. In March 1840 the Théâtre de la Renaissance accepted *Das Liebesverbot*, but the theatre was forced into bankruptcy two months later. There is no evidence to support Wagner's suggestion (made subsequently in *Mein Leben*) that Meyerbeer, through whose agency the work had been accepted, was aware of the imminent bankruptcy. Nor, apparently, did Wagner believe so at the time: on 20 September 1840 he wrote to Apel, 'Meyerbeer has remained untiringly loyal to my interests'. It is psychologically more plausible that Wagner's shameless obsequiousness before an influential patron was later transmuted by frustration and jealousy into the venomous bitterness seen, for example, in *Das Judentum in der Musik* (1850, rev. 1869).

In May 1840 Wagner sent Eugène Scribe a copy of his sketch of *Der fliegende Holländer*, and the following month he mentioned it to Meyerbeer, in the hope that he might use his influence to have the work put on at the Opéra. Meyerbeer introduced him to the new director of the Opéra, Léon Pillet, who bought the story for 500 francs, supposedly to have it made into an opera by one of the composers under contract to him. In fact, the two librettists given the sketch, Paul Foucher and Bénédict-Henry Révoil, did not, as generally stated, base their work *Le vaisseau fantâme* primarily on it but on a variety of sources including

Captain Marryat's *The Phantom Ship* and Sir Walter Scott's *The Pirate*. Wagner meanwhile proceeded to elaborate his scenario into a work of his own and initially he worked on the *Holländer* in tandem with *Rienzi*, which was completed in November 1840.

It was at this time that Wagner was threatened with imprisonment for debt, but the available evidence strongly suggests that the threat was never executed. Partly through Meyerbeer's influence, *Rienzi* was accepted by the Dresden Hoftheater. Preparations were under way by April 1842, when Wagner, deeply disillusioned with Paris, began to make his way back to the fatherland.

2. KAPELLMEISTER IN DRESDEN: 1843–9

The première of *Rienzi* on 20 October 1842 was an immense success, catching, as the work did, the rebellious spirit of the times. The darker, introspective quality of the *Holländer*, which followed at the Hoftheater on 2 January 1843, proved less appealing. Nevertheless, Wagner was an obvious candidate for the post of Kapellmeister at the King of Saxony's court in Dresden, which had become vacant at that time. The prospect of financial security finally outweighed any doubts he had about accepting a liveried post in the royal service. Technically, Wagner's status as second Kapellmeister was commensurate with that of the first Kapellmeister, Reissiger, but by the 1840s the latter was content to rest on his laurels while younger colleagues undertook the more onerous duties.

Those duties included conducting operatic, instrumental and orchestral performances and composing pieces for special court occasions. Among the latter works are numbered *Das Liebesmahl der Apostel* (1843), a biblical scene for male voices and orchestra; *Der Tag erscheint* (1843), a chorus for the unveiling of a monument to the king; *Gruss seiner Treuen an Friedrich August den Geliebten* (1844), another choral tribute to the king; and *An Webers Grabe* (1844), a chorus for the ceremony attending the reburial of Weber's remains in his home town (the campaign to effect which Wagner had vigorously supported).

Wagner had begun work on his next major project, *Tannhäuser*, in the summer of 1842, when a detailed prose draft was worked out at Aussig (now Ústí nad Labem) in the Bohemian mountains. It was not versified until the spring of the following year, and the composition occupied Wagner between July 1843 and April 1845. The first performance took place at the Hoftheater on 19 October 1845. Wagner then spent three months analysing the conditions under which court music was produced at Dresden. His proposals, including a series of winter orchestral concerts, were eminently reasonable, but after a year's delay Wagner was informed that they had been rejected.

Wagner's library in Dresden embraced a broad range of literature, both ancient and modern, from Calderón to Xenophon and from Gibbon to Molière. It also contained versions of Gottfried von Strassburg's *Tristan*, editions of the *Parzival* and *Lohengrin* epics, and a number of volumes on the medieval cobbler-poet Hans Sachs. The subjects of *Lohengrin* and each of the music dramas to follow the *Ring* were thus germinating in his mind during these years; a first prose draft was actually made for *Die Meistersinger* at Marienbad in 1845.

An event of major importance for Wagner was his organization in 1846 of a performance of Beethoven's Ninth Symphony (still at that time considered an unapproachable work) for the traditional Palm Sunday concert in the old opera house. Against considerable opposition from the administration he secured a notable financial and artistic success. The existence of sketches dating from 1846–7 for at least two symphonies bears witness to the inspirational effect the preparations for the Ninth had on Wagner himself.

During these years too he was working on the composition of *Lohengrin*, as well as studying Aeschylus (*Oresteia*), Aristophanes and other Greek authors in translation. In February 1847 he conducted his own arrangement of Gluck's *Iphigénie en Aulide*. His meagre salary (1500 talers per annum) was not enough to cover essential outgoings, but Minna managed the household efficiently and enjoyed the status of Kapellmeister's wife. They remained involuntarily childless (probably as a result of an earlier miscarriage) but in general the marriage was at its most stable at this period.

The insurrectionary outbreaks in Paris in February 1848 and in Vienna the following month were greeted with zealous approbation by the ranks of middle-class German liberals, indignant at the indifference of their princely rulers to social deprivation among the working classes, and motivated by fear of their own proletarianization. In Dresden barricades were erected and the king presented with demands for democratic reform. Wagner's plan for the organization of a German national theatre, which proposed that the director of such an institution be elected, that a drama school be set up, the court orchestra expanded and its administration put under self-management, was a reflection of such democratic principles, and consequently rejected. It is mistaken to see such a proposal – or, indeed, Wagner's involvement in the revolution generally – simply as opportunist. He naturally wished to see the role of the opera house enhanced in a reconstructed society, but such a desire sprang from the conviction that art was the highest and potentially most fruitful form of human endeavour.

He threw in his lot with the insurrectionists when in June 1848 he delivered a speech to the Vaterlandsverein, the leading republican grouping, on the subject of the relation of republican aspirations to the monarchy. The evils of money and speculation were denounced as barriers to the emancipation of the human race, and the downfall of the aristocracy was predicted. The notion that the Saxon king should remain at the head of the new republic, as 'the first and truest republican of all', was not an idiosyncratic one, but in tune with the limited demands of the bourgeois liberals for constitutional government.

Wagner remained for the time being at his post, and began to set down a prose résumé of what was to become the *Ring*. The manuscript, dated 4 October 1848, was headed *Die Nibelungensage (Mythus)*, though it was subsequently renamed *Der Nibelungen-Mythus: als Entwurf zu einem Drama*. A prose draft of *Siegfrieds Tod* (later to become *Götterdämmerung*) was made the same month, followed (not preceded, as previously supposed) by the essay *Die Wibelungen: Weltgeschichte aus der Sage* (winter 1848–9). Other projects of the period included *Friedrich I* (in five acts, possibly intended as a musical drama), *Jesus von Nazareth* (probably also intended as a five-act opera, though only a prose draft was completed), *Achilleus* (sketches for a work in three acts) and *Wieland der Schmied* (a heroic opera in three acts; prose draft). *Wieland* and, in particular, *Jesus von Nazareth* espouse the ideas of Pierre-Joseph Proudhon and Ludwig Feuerbach: ownership of property as the root of evil, supremacy of love over the law, and a new religion of humanity.

Wagner's assistant conductor, August Röckel, was no less of a firebrand, and the weekly republican journal he edited, the *Volksblätter*, contained various inflammatory tirades by Wagner and others. Through Röckel, Wagner came to know Mikhail Bakunin, the Russian anarchist, who in turn was acquainted personally with Marx and Engels. The fact that no works of Marx were contained in Wagner's library at Dresden provides no proof that Wagner was unfamiliar with his ideas: radical theories would have circulated freely in a major city such as Dresden.

Wagner's active role in the Dresden insurrection obliged him to flee for his life when the Prussian troops began to gain control in May 1849. He was sheltered by Liszt at Weimar before making his way on a false passport to Switzerland. A warrant had been issued for his arrest.

3. COMPOSER IN EXILE: 1849–63

ZÜRICH ESSAYS

Even after the savage crushing of the 1848–9 uprisings, Wagner continued to believe that both social and artistic reform were imminent. In the first years of his exile in Zürich – he was not to enter Germany again until 1860 – he formulated a set of aesthetic theories intended to establish opera in a radically recast form as at once the instrument and the product of a reconstructed society. In the first of this series of Zürich essays, *Die Kunst und die Revolution* (1849), written under the influence of Proudhon and Feuerbach, Wagner outlined the debasement of art since the era of the glorious, all-embracing Greek drama. Only when art was liberated from the sphere of capitalist speculation and profit-making would it be able to express the spirit of emancipated humanity. The vehicle envisaged to effect this transformation process, namely the 'art-work of the future', was elaborated, along with the concept of the reunification of the arts into a comprehensive *Gesamtkunstwerk* ('total work of art') on the ancient Greek model, in two further essays, *Das Kunstwerk der Zukunft* (1849) and *Oper und Drama* (1850–51).

In the former, Wagner argued that the elements of dance, music and poetry, harmonized so perfectly in Greek drama, were deprived of their expressive potential when divorced from each other. In the 'art-work of the future' they would be reunited both with each other (in the 'actor of the future', at once dancer, musician and poet) and with the arts of architecture, sculpture and painting. Allowance was even made for the occasional use of the spoken word. Theatres would need to be redesigned by aesthetic criteria rather than those of social hierarchy. Landscape painters would be required to execute the sets. Above all, the new work of art was to be created, in response to a communal need, by a fellowship of artists, representative of *das Volk* ('the people').

The philosophical basis of *Das Kunstwerk der Zukunft* is multi-faceted. The *völkisch* ideology, which urged a return to a remote primordial world where peasants of true Germanic blood lived as a true community, had evolved with the rise of national consciousness in the 18th century. Notions such as that of the *Volk's* creative endeavours arising spontaneously out of sheer necessity – a process of historical inevitability – owe much to Feuerbach and to such revolutionary thinkers as Marx. Nor was the concept of the *Gesamtkunstwerk* new: writers such as Lessing, Novalis, Tieck, Schelling and Hoffmann had previously advocated, either in theory or in practice, some sort of reunification of the arts, while the idea of the regeneration of art in accordance with classical ideals can be identified with Winckelmann, Wieland, Lessing, Goethe and Schiller.

Oper und Drama is an immense discourse on the aesthetics of drama-through-music. A new form of verse-setting (*Versmelodie*) is outlined, in which the melody will grow organically out of the verse. It will use *Stabreim* (an old German verse form using alliteration) and a system of presentiments and reminiscences, functioning as *melodische Momente* ('melodic impulses'). Only rarely will one voice serve as harmonic support for another; choruses and other ensembles will be eliminated. Wagner's claim that the new ideas and techniques had 'already matured' within him before the theory was formulated is something of an exaggeration, as is suggested by his willingness to adapt the theoretical principles in the light of practical experience. Their formulation did, however, enable him to grapple with the central issue: how to reconcile his own fundamentally literary and dramatic inspirations with the Classical symphonic tradition.

Two other important essays of the period should be mentioned. *Das Judentum in der Musik* argues that the superficial, meretricious values of contemporary art are embodied, above all, in Jewish musicians. The rootlessness of Jews in Germany and their historical role as usurers and entrepreneurs has condemned them, in Wagner's view, to cultural sterility. The uncompromisingly anti-Semitic tone of the essay was, in part, provoked by repeated allegations that Wagner was indebted artistically, as well as financially, to Meyerbeer. The preoccupations and prejudices of *Das Judentum* also place it in an anti-Jewish tradition, often of otherwise impeccably liberal and humanitarian credentials, going back via Luther to the Middle Ages. Even the idea that Jews should, as part of the process of assimilation, undergo a programme of re-education was not novel, though the refinement (stated elsewhere) that that education programme should largely consist of the Wagnerian music drama was original.

In 1851 Wagner wrote an extensive preface to accompany the projected publication of the librettos of the *Holländer*, *Tannhäuser* and *Lohengrin*. This autobiographical essay, called *Eine Mitteilung an meine Freunde*, is of interest for the insights it offers into Wagner's own view of his life and works to that date.

LIFE IN EXILE

In Zürich Wagner made the acquaintance of a number of cultured individuals, some of whom provided pecuniary as well as intellectual sustenance. A pair of female admirers, Julie Ritter, a widow from Dresden, and Jessie Laussot (née Taylor), an Englishwoman married to a Bordeaux wine merchant, jointly offered him an annual allowance of 3000 francs (equivalent to 800 talers, or approximately half his Dresden salary) for an indefinite period. Such benefactors showed the kind of disinterested generosity and confidence in his artistic endeavours that he found lacking in his wife, Minna, whose constant reproaches he found increasingly hard to bear. A love affair between Wagner and Jessie (who, according to him, was also unhappily married) briefly blossomed. When, on the intervention of Jessie's mother and death threats from her husband, it ended, one source of financial support dried up. But an unexpected legacy then enabled Julie Ritter to confer the full amount herself, which she continued to do from 1851 to 1859.

Lohengrin received its world première at Weimar under Liszt, with the composer necessarily absent. A drastic water cure at nearby Albisbrunn failed to relieve the dual complaints of erysipelas (a skin disease) and severe constipation, and further depression resulted from the failure of the revolution to materialize in France, or elsewhere in Europe. Several of Wagner's letters of the period speak of a loveless, cheerless existence; more than once he contemplated suicide.

By February 1853 he was able to recite the completed text of the *Ring* to an invited audience at the Hotel Baur au Lac in Zürich; 50 copies of the poem were printed at his own expense. Financial assistance from Otto Wesendonck, a retired silk merchant to whom Wagner had been introduced early in 1852, allowed him to present and conduct three concerts of excerpts from his works (May 1853) and to make a trip to Italy. Wagner's account (in *Mein Leben*) of the dream-inspired onrush of inspiration for *Das Rheingold* while he lay half-asleep in a hotel room in La Spezia has been dismissed as a further example of mythification (Deathridge and Dahlhaus, H 1984), though it has been argued (Darcy, N 1993) that the documentary evidence neither supports nor contradicts Wagner's account. The story bears witness, in any case, to the perceived importance of the new artistic phase being entered, and it was indeed in the succeeding months that the music of the *Ring* began to take shape.

In September 1854 Wagner reckoned his debts at 10,000 francs – by this time he was supporting not only Minna and her illegitimate daughter Natalie, but also Minna's parents. Wesendonck agreed to settle most of these in exchange for the receipts from future performances of Wagner's works. Appeals for clemency made on his behalf to the new King of Saxony, Johann, were rejected, no doubt on the advice of the Dresden police, whose agents still had Wagner under surveillance. Several of his acquaintances were regarded as dangerous political refugees, not least Georg Herwegh. Ironically it was Herwegh who in September or October 1854 introduced him to the quietist, renunciatory philosophy that was so to influence his future outlook on life: that of Arthur Schopenhauer.

Schopenhauer's influence was twofold: his philosophy (which had many parallels with Buddhist thinking), advocating the denial of the will and consequent release from the cycle of suffering, was profoundly to affect the ideological orientation – and even the locution – of each of Wagner's remaining dramatic works. Schopenhauer's aesthetics, which elevated music above the other arts, made a similarly forceful impact. But Wagner's abandonment of the concept of the egalitarian co-existence of the arts should be seen not so much as a wholesale *volte face* from *Oper und Drama* principles as a shift of emphasis from the realization of those principles in *Rheingold* and *Walküre*.

An invitation from the Philharmonic Society to conduct a series of eight concerts in London resulted in a four-month stay in England in 1855. A hostile press campaign, the uncongenial weather and the philistinism of the English combined to make the visit an unhappy one. On returning to Zürich he completed his severely disrupted work on *Walküre* (1856) and made a short prose sketch for an opera on a Buddhist subject: *Die Sieger*. The latter project was never completed, but its themes – passion and chastity, renunciation and redemption – were later subsumed into *Parsifal*.

Otto Wesendonck put at Wagner's disposal a small house adjacent to the villa he was having built in the Enge suburb of Zürich. Wagner and Minna moved in at the end of April 1857 and Wesendonck and his wife Mathilde to their own home in August. A love affair developed between Wagner and Mathilde, though their love – celebrated and idealized in *Tristan und Isolde* – was probably never consummated. To begin work on *Tristan* (20 August 1857) Wagner abandoned *Siegfried*, returning to sustained work on it only in 1869. An eruption of marital strife necessitated Wagner's move out of the 'Asyl' (as, following Mathilde's suggestion, he had called the little house). In the company of Karl Ritter he travelled to Venice; the second act of *Tristan* was completed there (in draft) on 1 July 1858 and the third act in Lucerne on 16 July 1859.

Preparing another offensive against Paris, Wagner conducted, at the beginning of 1860 in the Théâtre Italien, three concerts of excerpts from his works. Through the intervention of Princess Pauline Metternich *Tannhäuser* was eventually staged at the Opéra on 13 March 1861; a politically inspired demonstration, combined with Wagner's refusal to supply the customary second-act ballet, caused a débâcle and the production was withdrawn after three severely disrupted performances. A partial amnesty (Saxony remained barred until the following March) allowed Wagner to return to Germany on 12 August 1860.

In February 1862 he took lodgings in Biebrich, near Mainz, and set to work on the composition of *Die Meistersinger von Nürnberg*, for which he had made two further prose drafts (elaborating that of 1845) the previous November. Surrounded as he now was by female admirers, he yet baulked, on compassionate grounds, at putting a decisive end to his irreparably broken marriage. Instead, he installed Minna, with a not ungenerous allowance, in Dresden; they last met in November 1862 and Minna died in January 1866.

Renting the upper floor of a house in Penzing, near Vienna, in May 1863, he furnished it in luxurious style, heedless of the consequences. His generosity to friends was equally unstinting and by March the following year he was obliged to leave Vienna under threat of arrest for debt.

4. MUNICH AND BAYREUTH: 1864–77

A plea for pecuniary assistance published by Wagner along with the *Ring* poems in 1863 was answered in spectacular fashion when a new monarch ascended the throne of Bavaria in March 1864. The 18-year-old Ludwig II discharged Wagner's immediate debts, awarded him an annual stipend of 4000 gulden (comparable to that of a ministerial councillor) and continued his support for many years, making possible the first Bayreuth festivals of 1876 and 1882.

A plea to Mathilde Maier to join him in the Villa Pellet, his new home over-looking Lake Starnberg, was less successful. But by now Wagner was on intimate terms with Cosima von Bülow, Liszt's daughter, unsuitably married to the conductor Hans von Bülow, and their union was consummated some time between the arrival at Starnberg of Cosima (with two daughters and nurserymaid) on 29 June 1864 and that of Hans on 7 July. The child that resulted, Isolde, was born on 10 April 1865.

In October 1864 a more spacious house at 21 Briennerstrasse in Munich was made available to Wagner by Ludwig; it was decked out extravagantly, as was Wagner himself, in silks and satins supplied by a Viennese seamstress. When Ludwig summoned Gottfried Semper to Munich to design a Wagnerian festival theatre, local vested interests opposed the scheme. Difficulties were also encountered with Franz von Pfistermeister and Ludwig von der Pfordten, respectively Ludwig's cabinet secretary and prime minister, and eventually there was resentment from the court circles and populace generally. Wagner's proposal for a music school to be established in Munich, appropriate for the nature of German music and drama, was seen as opportunistic, and Ludwig's support of the première of *Tristan* at the Hof- und Nationaltheater merely fuelled the hostility that accompanied the work's unveiling to a bemused public.

Castigation of Wagner for 'cynical exploitation' of Ludwig can be overplayed. It is true that he was as skilled at manipulating people in real life as in his dramas, and that he seized the opportunity to acquire the domestic comforts he had been so long denied. But his overriding concern was to obtain the best possible conditions for his art. And as Manfred Eger (I 1986) has pointed out, the total amount received by Wagner from Ludwig over the 19 years of their acquaintance – including stipend, rent and the cash value of presents – was 562,914 marks, a sum equivalent to less than one-seventh of the yearly Civil List (4.2 million marks). It is a sum that also compares modestly with the 652,000 marks spent on the bed-chamber alone of Ludwig's castle of Herrenchiemsee, or with the 1.7 million marks spent on the bridal carriage for the royal wedding that never took place.

Ludwig, however, recognized that his close association with Wagner was costing him popular support, and in December 1865 reluctantly instructed him to leave Munich. Accompanied by Cosima, Wagner discovered and acquired a house called Tribschen (or Triebschen, to adopt Wagner's idiosyncratic spelling) overlooking Lake Lucerne. His cohabitation with Cosima (permanent from October 1868) was initially concealed from Ludwig and a scandal-mongering article in the Munich *Volksbote* drove the couple to blind the king with a charade of lamentable mendacity.

From Tribschen Wagner continued to offer Ludwig the political advice with which he had always been generous. Now that Bavaria was caught up in the war between Prussia and Austria, Wagner's opinion, strongly influenced by the views of the conservative federalist Constantin Frantz, was that Bavaria should remain neutral. Bavaria, however, sided with Austria; its defeat not only enabled Prussian hegemony to be established, but also brought about the collapse of the German Confederation.

The impact on Wagner of Frantz's views was crucial to the ideological background of *Meistersinger* as it took shape during the 1860s. Schopenhauer's ethic of renunciation had by now given way to a more positive, more nationalistic outlook, reflecting the mood of optimism in the country at large arising from Germany's increasing industrial growth, national wealth and social cohesion, coupled with the rise of Bismarck. In *Was ist deutsch?* (1865), written for the private edification of the king, Wagner articulated the concern of many members of the middle class for traditional German values, apparently under threat. The divided religion effected by the Reformation, and the near-collapse of the German race, have led to an invasion by 'an utterly alien element', namely the Jews. The result is a 'repugnant caricature of the German spirit', which, according to Wagner, is beautiful and noble, not motivated by profit or self-interest.

Shortly after *Was ist deutsch?* was written, Wagner received a letter from Frantz telling him that in his music he had recognized 'the fundamental chord of German being'. A subsequent essay, *Deutsche Kunst und deutsche Politik* (1867), endorses Frantz's assertion that it is the 'mission' of Germany to forge a 'nobler culture, against which French civilization will no longer have any power', and goes on to propose that German art is a manifestation of that indomitable 'German spirit' which alone is capable of steering Germany and its politics through these difficult days. *Meistersinger* is the artistic component of Wagner's ideological crusade of the 1860s: a crusade to revive the 'German spirit' and purge it of alien elements.

The première of *Meistersinger* on 21 June 1868 was a triumph for Wagner. At Ludwig's insistence, but to Wagner's dismay when he realized how inadequate the performances would be, *Rheingold* and *Walküre* were also staged in Munich in 1869 and 1870 respectively. A second child, Eva, had been born to Wagner and Cosima on 17 February 1867, and after the birth of the third, Siegfried, on 6 June 1869, Cosima asked her husband for a divorce; Bülow immediately agreed, though Cosima's marriage to Wagner could not take place until 25 August 1870.

Wagner's anti-Gallic sympathies were given their head when in July 1870 war broke out between France and Prussia (supported by the south German states, including Bavaria). His farce, *Eine Kapitulation*, making tasteless capital out of the suffering endured by the Parisians during the siege of their city, returned to a favourite theme: the swamping of German culture by frivolous French art.

In the essay *Beethoven*, published in 1870 to coincide with the centenary celebrations of the composer, Wagner completed a process of rapprochement, initiated with '*Zukunftsmusik*' ten years earlier, between the aesthetics of *Oper und Drama* and those of Schopenhauer. In '*Zukunftsmusik*' Wagner continued to elevate his own species of text-related musical discourse above pure instrumental music, but the claim is modified by a reappraisal of the worth of symphonic music, particularly that of Beethoven. In *Beethoven* he finally accepts that words and music cannot enjoy totally equal status: with Schopenhauer, he maintains that music is the ultimate vehicle of expression. However, the union of music and words does permit a range of emotional expression far wider than that yielded by each alone. As Carl Dahlhaus has pointed out, Wagner returned, with this formulation, to something akin to the traditional Romantic conception of the aesthetic of music which he had espoused about 1840, long before his encounter with Schopenhauer.

Settling on the Upper Franconian town of Bayreuth for his planned festival enterprise, Wagner began to secure the support both of the local authorities and of 'patrons' across the country. The foundation stone of the theatre was laid on 22 May 1872 (Wagner's birthday); Beethoven's Ninth Symphony was performed. Wagner and Cosima moved to a temporary home in Bayreuth, and then, in April 1874, into 'Wahnfried'. The first festival, announced for 1873, had already been postponed for lack of funds. After an unsuccessful appeal to the Reich, the enterprise was saved only by a loan of 100,000 talers from Ludwig. Admission tickets would have to be sold, however, in contravention of Wagner's original ideal of free access for the populace.

The score of *Götterdämmerung* was completed on 21 November 1874; rehearsals were initiated in the summer of the following year. The part of Siegfried went not to Albert Niemann, Wagner's Paris Tannhäuser, but to the untried Georg Unger, who required close supervision from a singing teacher. The Brünnhilde, Amalie Materna from Vienna, also had to be coached, though the Wotan, Franz Betz, having sung the Munich Hans Sachs, was more familiar with Wagner's demands. In charge of movement and gesture on the stage was Richard Fricke, Wagner retaining overall control of the direction; his instructions were recorded in detail by Heinrich Porges. There were three cycles, beginning on 13 August 1876, attended by musicians, critics and notables from all over Europe. The reaction, predictably, was mixed, admiration for the realization of such an enterprise being tempered by criticism of details. Wagner himself was far from satisfied with the staging, which he vowed to revise in future years; nor were the tempos of the conductor, Hans Richter, to his liking.

An intimacy with the French writer Judith Gautier continued from the time of the 1876 festival until February 1878, when it was brought firmly but diplomatically to a halt by Cosima. A scarcely less intense relationship with Friedrich

Nietzsche continued from 1869, when the latter first visited Tribschen, until Nietzsche's so-called 'second period' (1876–82), when he turned against art as romantic illusion and excoriated Wagner for betraying what he had identified as his challenging, affirmative spirit.

In the hope of discharging the deficit of the festival (148,000 marks) Wagner undertook a series of concerts in the newly opened Royal Albert Hall in London. He was well received, but the net profits of £700 (approximately 14,300 marks) were disappointingly low, thanks to miscalculations by the inexperienced agents.

5. THE FINAL YEARS: 1878–83

'REGENERATION' WRITINGS

In January 1878 appeared the first issue of the *Bayreuther Blätter*, a journal devoted to the Wagnerian cause, set up by Wagner under the editorship of Hans von Wolzogen. Its viewpoint was described, by Wagner, as 'the decline of the human race and the need for the establishment of a system of ethics'. That 'system of ethics' was expounded in the series of essays known as the 'regeneration' writings, beginning with *Modern* (1878) and ending with *Heldentum und Christentum* (1881). The salient themes are as follows. The human species has degenerated by abandoning its original, natural vegetable diet, and absorbing the corrupted blood of slaughtered animals. Regeneration may be effected only by a return to natural food and it must be rooted in the soil of a true religion. Even the most degenerate races may be purified by the untainted blood of Christ, received in the sacrament of the Eucharist. The miscegenation of the pure Aryan race with the Jews has also contributed to the degeneration of the species.

The last notion Wagner owed to Count Joseph-Arthur de Gobineau, whose acquaintance in these years he greatly valued. Their respective philosophies diverged, however, in as much as Gobineau held that miscegenation was a necessary evil for the continuation of civilization, whereas in Wagner's more optimistic view the human race was redeemable by Christ's blood. Racialist philosophies of this kind were rampant in Wilhelminian Germany. With the unification finally achieved in 1871, there had emerged an industrial bourgeoisie that usurped the privileged position of the former liberal nationalists who had struggled for it. Wagner was one of many whose allegiance shifted from liberalism to a form of romantic conservatism. A new wave of anti-Semitic sentiment swept Germany, if anything intensified rather than tempered by the emancipation legislation of the early 1870s. This is the ideological background against which *Parsifal* was written.

15

LAST YEARS

The Bayreuth deficit was eventually cleared by an agreement, dated 31 March 1878, according to which Wagner confirmed Ludwig's right to produce all his works in the Hoftheater without payment, the king voluntarily setting aside 10% of all such receipts until the deficit was discharged. In a further clause, Wagner agreed that the first performance of *Parsifal* (either in Bayreuth or Munich) should be given with the orchestra, singers and artistic personnel of the Hoftheater, after which Munich was to have unrestricted rights over the work. It was this clause that compelled Wagner to accept the Jewish Hermann Levi as the conductor of *Parsifal* in 1882.

In August 1879 Wagner responded to an appeal for his support in a campaign against vivisection by writing a sympathetic open letter to Ernst von Weber on the subject. However, he refused to sign Bernhard Förster's 'Mass Petition against the Rampancy of Judaism', partly out of self-interest and partly out of a preference for addressing the issue in a more theoretical manner. In the early 1880s his health began to deteriorate: cardiac spasms were followed by a major heart attack in March 1882. After the second Bayreuth festival, consisting of 16 performances of *Parsifal* in July and August 1882, Wagner and his family took up residence in the Palazzo Vendramin, Venice. His final, fatal heart attack occurred there on 13 February 1883, following an uncharacteristically bitter row with Cosima, apparently provoked by the announcement of a visit from one of the *Parsifal* flowermaidens, Carrie Pringle, with whom it has been alleged Wagner may have been unduly intimate. His body was taken in a draped gondola to the railway station, from where it was conveyed to Bayreuth. The burial was a private ceremony held in the grounds of Wahnfried.

6. WRITINGS

Few composers can ever have devoted so much time to the written word as Wagner. His essays, gathered alongside the poems for his dramatic works in the 16 volumes of collected writings, cover a wide range of subjects. Those dealing with aesthetics and social and political issues have already been considered in the biographical section.

JOURNALISM

The main body of Wagner's journalistic writings dates from his Paris years (1839–42). Finding that artistic success was slower in coming than he had anticipated, Wagner turned his hand to journalism – as to the making of hack arrangements – in an attempt to stave off penury. Maurice Schlesinger, the publisher of the *Revue et Gazette musicale*, provided him with both. In addition to the *Revue* (where his articles appeared in French translation), Wagner wrote for the journal *Europa*, published in Stuttgart by August Lewald, Schumann's *Neue Zeitschrift für Musik*, and the Dresden *Abend-Zeitung*.

Wagner's initial reason for turning to journalism may have been financial, but – like Berlioz – he soon developed a flair for it. In fact, although his novellas, such as *Eine Pilgerfahrt zu Beethoven* and *Ein Ende in Paris*, are in the style of E.T.A. Hoffmann, the music criticism – for all that its satirical tone seems to be modelled on Heine's – is closer to that of Berlioz, at that time the leading musical commentator in Paris. The preoccupations of the two composers are remarkably similar, reflecting both a disdain for the commercial imperatives driving contemporary artistic life and an idealistic vision of a society in which art was accorded its true place.

Eine Pilgerfahrt zu Beethoven is a humorous, fictional account of a visit by a young composer to Beethoven in Vienna. The element of autobiographical wish-fulfilment is evident not only in the designation of the young composer ('R...' from 'L...') but in the imputing to Beethoven of aesthetic principles identifiable as the incipient music drama. Thus the choral finale of the Ninth Symphony is characterized as a transition from abstract symphonic music to a new genre of 'musical drama', eschewing arias, duets, terzettos and the like in favour of a radical synthesis of vocal and instrumental categories.

In *Ein Ende in Paris*, the Beethoven-worshipping 'R...' from the previous novella is starving to death in Paris (a scenario that only marginally exaggerates Wagner's personal situation). The triviality of present-day music-making in the French capital is excoriated in a defiant artistic credo: 'I believe in God, Mozart and Beethoven, and also in their disciples and apostles ... I believe in a Day of Judgment, upon which all those who presumed to make extortionate profits in this world from such sublime, pure art ... will be fearfully punished. I believe that they will be condemned to listen to their own music for all eternity.' Humour and piquant irony are salient features of these novellas – a lightness of touch that deserted Wagner in his later prose writings – and it is even conceivable (Weiner, I 1995) that the philistine, mercantilist Englishman in these stories is modelled on Schlesinger. A third novella, *Ein glücklicher Abend*, also deals with Beethoven and the boundaries of abstract music.

A group of essays addressing aesthetic questions introduces a significant polemical note in its appeal to national difference. *Über deutsches Musikwesen* suggests that instrumental music is the domain of the Germans, whereas vocal music is that of the Italians. In a word: 'the Italian is a singer, the Frenchman a virtuoso, the German – a musician'. That is to say, the German supposedly loves music for its own sake, not as a means of delighting an audience or making a reputation. Adumbrated here is the notion of German art as uniquely true, profound and spiritual, in contrast to latinate culture, which is superficial and concerned with display. *Der Virtuos und der Künstler*, comparing the artistry of a Grisi or a Lablache with the virtuosity of Rubini, mocks the latter's preposterous trilling on a high A–B♮ in *Don Giovanni*, launched like a trapeze artist and received like a circus act by a stunned audience. *Der Künstler und die Öffentlichkeit* depicts the humiliations the true artist has to endure in presenting his work to the public. The principles enunciated here, often in satirical form – the idealist struggle against the debased values of contemporary musical life, the authenticity of true German artistic feeling, the threat posed by foreign (specifically Franco-Jewish) influence – were to inform the writings, and indeed the operas, of Wagner throughout his life.

Wagner's essays on music and musical life from this period have to be read against the background of their intended audience. When writing for the *Revue et Gazette musicale*, Wagner was addressing the Parisian musical establishment that held the key to his own fortunes in that city. Moreover, the journal's publisher, Schlesinger, had a vested interest in promoting those composers – primarily Meyerbeer and Halévy – whose works provided him with a major source of income. As a result – and the *Revue* was, of course, far from unique in this respect – criticism of such house composers tended to be muted. A comparison of Wagner's two articles on Halévy's *La reine de Chypre* – that for the *Revue* in February/May 1841, and that for the Dresden *Abend-Zeitung* shortly before (26/29 January) – is indicative of the constraints under which he was working. Wagner's criticism of the work is that, for all its incidental beauties and often impressive effects, *La reine* is compromised by its libretto, which lacks the compelling poetic quality of *La Juive*. In his report for the *Abend-Zeitung*, Wagner deals with this perceived failing at considerable length, mentioning the music only in passing. His *Revue* article, by contrast, deals with the music at much greater length and is far more complimentary. Wagner even adopts here the persona of a French writer, describing the Opéra as 'our great lyric stage', which will one day be open to 'true talents', when 'all those who have at heart the interests of great and true musical drama will take Halévy as their model'. Wagner's admiration for aspects of Halévy's art was doubtless genuine; indeed, he retained it throughout his life. But whereas the *Revue* critique reflects its proprietor's interests as well as revealing Wagner's own ambitions, the *Abend-Zeitung* article probably expresses with more honesty his disappointment at the opera's shortcomings.

The *La reine* review is contained in a series of reports filed to the Dresden *Abend-Zeitung* in 1841, in which Wagner comments acerbically – though giving credit where he believed it due – on musical life in Paris. His review of the production of Weber's *Der Freischütz* at the Opéra, for example (16/21 July

1841), deplores the practice of adding recitatives (spoken dialogue not being allowed at the Opéra), but Wagner acknowledges that the man employed to commit this desecration – Berlioz, no less – probably did less damage than many others might have done. In an earlier essay (14/17 June 1841) Wagner describes his reaction to the *Symphonie fantastique* and *Roméo et Juliette*. They were, he considered, rich in inspiration and imagination; flawed but the work of a genius. Significantly, Wagner's appraisal of Berlioz is coloured by his prejudices about national identity. In that he does not write for material gain, Berlioz is held to be uncharacteristic of the French. But the lapses of taste and artistic blemishes Wagner perceives alongside passages of pure genius in *Roméo et Juliette* are, he considers, the result of an internal conflict. Berlioz is an essentially private artist, dedicated to exploring the profound and mysterious depths of his inner being; yet his audience, irredeemably French as they are, expect to be entertained. Thus, according to Wagner, Berlioz instinctively attempts, against his true nature, to create effects with which he might 'stupefy and conquer the gaping crowd'.

DIARIES

Given Wagner's concern that he be accorded an appropriate place in history, it is scarcely surprising that he should at various times have kept – or in latter years ensured that his wife kept – a diary to provide raw material for future biographers. His first systematic attempt to log the events of his life is contained in the so-called 'Red Pocketbook', a volume begun in August 1835, when Wagner was scouting for singers for Heinrich Bethmann's Magdeburg-based travelling theatre company. The sketchy notes of this 'diary' were continued until the winter of 1865–6, by which time Wagner had begun to dictate his autobiography *Mein Leben* to Cosima (17 July 1865), drawing on them as an *aide-mémoire*. That they were also intended to serve some biographical purpose is clear from the fact that the notes begin by sketching in the salient details of Wagner's life and work from his birth to the present day. The succinctness of the notes – frequently just a name or a place, or a phrase such as 'whips, pistols', for the furious pursuit of his recently absconded wife, Minna, with the merchant Dietrich – often requires cross-checking with some other biographical source to provide elucidation. Only the first four sides of the 'Red Pocketbook' have survived, taking the story to 17 September 1839. These pages were reproduced, with annotation, in volume i of the *Sämtliche Briefe*.

Only three entries have survived of another diary kept by Wagner – a record of his experiences in Paris in the summer of 1840, when he was reduced to penury – namely those for 23, 29 and 30 June (reproduced in volume xvi of the *Sämtliche Schriften*). The function served by the 'Red Pocketbook', on the other hand, was continued by the so-called Annals, which take up the story from Easter 1846 and continue it up to the end of 1867. These Annals, which were transferred at a later date to the 'Brown Book' (a leather-bound notebook given to Wagner by Cosima in 1864 or 1865), were apparently subjected to a certain amount of editing during that process. Wagner's predisposition to mythologize the conception of his major works – perhaps exacerbated in the editing by the epigrammatic brevity of some of the entries – requires the exercising of considerable caution in drawing on the Annals for information relating to the genesis of such works. Sketch studies have suggested that the genesis of *Das Rheingold*, for example, is rather more complex than is intimated by the account of the La Spezia 'dream inspiration' here (Deathridge, N 1977, and Darcy, N 1993), while the implication that *Parsifal* was conceived on the Good Friday of 1857 has long been refuted. The Annals for the relevant period (1864–8) were published by Otto Strobel in his edition of Wagner's correspondence with King Ludwig II (Strobel, D 1936–9). The Annals were first published complete in Joachim Bergfeld's edition of the 'Brown Book' (A 1975). Between 21 August 1858 and 4 April 1859 Wagner kept another diary for a quite different purpose. This was the 'Venice Diary' – or, to give it Wagner's full title: *Tagebuch seit meiner Flucht aus dem Asyl 17. August 1858*. Having been obliged to leave the 'Asyl', adjacent to the Wesendonck villa in the Enge suburb of Zürich, on account of the embarrassment caused by his intimacy with Mathilde, Wagner kept a diary, to which he confided his feelings for her. He had been discouraged from communicating with Mathilde during this sojourn in Venice and she had returned his letters unopened. The 'Venice Diary' takes the form of a series of letters, but they were sent to their recipient not at the time of writing, but in two instalments, the first on 12 October 1858 and the second the following April. The 'Venice Diary' is interesting for its elaboration of the philosophical themes of fellow-suffering, renunciation and redemption, particularly in relation to *Parsifal*, characters and scenes of which were evidently taking shape in the composer's mind at this time. The text was published by Wolfgang Golther in his edition of Wagner's correspondence with Mathilde Wesendonck (D 1904). Between 14 and 27 September 1865 Wagner kept a journal in which he set down his thoughts on political issues for the benefit of King Ludwig II. The thrust of these reflections was that the German princes had lost touch with their people; the role of Ludwig was to lead his subjects once again to a true understanding of nationhood and cultural responsibility. This journal was published, in part, under the title *Was ist deutsch?* in the *Bayreuther Blätter* (1878) and subsequently in the collected writings.

If the journal for Ludwig scarcely constitutes a diary in the conventional sense, nor does the 'Brown Book'. Nevertheless, Wagner made use of Cosima's calf-bound gift in such diverse ways – it contains sketches, essays, poems and outlines of works in addition to the aforementioned Annals – as to render it an indispensable primary source. The original purpose of the book was to enable Wagner to address himself intimately to Cosima at a time when they were frequently forced apart. The first section of the book served that purpose, but between February 1866 and April 1867 they were together for most of the time at their new house Tribschen on Lake Lucerne, and the entries in the 'Brown Book' were temporarily discontinued. The final entry addressed to Cosima is a telegram of 17 February 1868 (the first birthday of their second daughter, Eva).

Among the most interesting items in the 'Brown Book' are the following: the first prose sketch for *Parsifal*; sketches for 'a Luther drama' and for the farcical play *Eine Kapitulation*; musical sketches entitled '*Romeo u. Julie*' and '*Sylvester 68–69*' (the latter a cradle song subsequently used in the *Siegfried Idyll*); and a series of jottings on culture and race related to the 'Regeneration Writings' of the last years.

The 'Brown Book' was entrusted by Cosima to Eva, who in turn presented it, after her mother's death, to the town of Bayreuth, with the wish that it be kept in the Richard-Wagner-Gedenkstätte. Regrettably, however, Eva (who married the English historian Houston Stewart Chamberlain in 1908) had seen fit to cut out and destroy seven pages (14 sides), pasting over a further five sides to render the contents illegible – the latter were subsequently recovered. The censored pages contain uncharacteristically ill-tempered remarks aimed at Cosima, Liszt, Gottfried Semper and King Ludwig II.

By far the most important source in this category are the diaries kept by Cosima from 1 January 1869 to the penultimate day of Wagner's life (12 February 1883). Recording, as they do, the minutiae of Wagner's life and thought processes, they represent not only an invaluable tool for Wagner scholarship but also an unparalleled documentation of bourgeois life of the period. The diaries consist of 21 identically bound volumes (black cardboard covers secured by green ribbons). None of the pages has been removed or pasted over, though in a few places whole sentences have been crossed out and rendered illegible, probably by Eva Chamberlain (they have been restored in the published edition, edited by Martin Gregor-Dellin and Dietrich Mack, A 1976–7).

The diaries were presented by Cosima to Eva, or so the latter swore on oath, as part of her dowry. At the time of her wedding the diaries were in Riga, where they were being consulted by Carl Friedrich Glasenapp for the final volume of his official biography of Wagner. They entered her possession in October 1911 and remained there until 1935, when she presented them to the city of Bayreuth, 'as a gift to the Richard-Wagner-Gedenkstätte'. Among her conditions for the gift was one that the distinguished Wagner scholar Otto Strobel should never be employed by the Gedenkstätte. (It was Strobel who had reported the loss of correspondence between Wagner and Cosima to the police. Eva subsequently admitted that she was responsible, asserting on oath that she had burned the letters shortly after the death of her brother Siegfried in 1930 and on his explicit wishes.) In her will of 28 April 1939 Eva further stipulated that Strobel never be allowed to see the diaries, and that they be deposited in a bank (the Bayerischer Staatsbank in Munich) until 30 years after her death. After further legal delay following the expiry of the embargo in 1972, the diaries finally entered the public domain on 12 March 1974, when they were transferred, under police escort, from the bank in Munich to Bayreuth.

While for Wagner the diaries provided an intimate and reliable record of the events of his everyday life, for Cosima they served as a confessional. Addressed to her children, they were intended to make it possible for them to understand why she had left Hans von Bülow in favour of Wagner. Wracked by a guilty conscience, Cosima interpreted every misfortune as a punishment (accepted willingly) for sinful behaviour. Her penitential self-mortification is the obverse of her slavish adulation of Wagner, and both are exemplified on every page, as is an obsessive, but revealingly casual, anti-Semitism.

The immense value of the diaries is twofold. On a simple biographical level, they confirm or correct data regarding multifarious aspects of Wagner and his works. But no less importantly, they also offer us the kind of 'fly-on-the-wall' observation of the composer and his immediate environment that enables every reader to construct for him- or herself an image of Wagner as a social being. Thus his occasional bouts of irritability can be seen alongside the discomfort caused by his bodily complaints and insomnia, his well-publicized self-centredness alongside striking demonstrations of generosity.

AUTOBIOGRAPHIES

The diary notes Wagner began in 1835 (the 'Red Pocketbook') for a future autobiography are described above. But the first of his published autobiographical writings was the *Autobiographische Skizze*, which appeared in Heinrich Laube's Leipzig journal *Zeitung für die elegante Welt*, in two instalments, on 1 and 8 February 1843, prefaced with an introduction by Laube. This was the period of Wagner's first major productions in Dresden – *Der fliegende Holländer* had been given on 2 January and *Rienzi* the previous October – and Laube's purpose was to profile the newcomer for the German public. In the *Autobiographische Skizze* Wagner describes, in some detail, the events of his life from his birth in Leipzig in 1813 to the time of his return to Germany (from Paris) in April 1842. The tone is lighthearted and dilettantish, blending the confidence of an ambitious young man with a touch of self-deprecatory candour regarding his juvenilia.

Wagner's next autobiographical essay, *Eine Mitteilung an meine Freunde*, was written to introduce the librettos of his three Romantic operas – *Der fliegende*

Holländer, *Tannhäuser* and *Lohengrin* – on their publication in December 1851. Concerned that he had been 'misunderstood' in his artistic intentions, he wished, he told his friends, to clarify them. *Eine Mitteilung* thus describes and offers interpretative insights into those operas, as well as mentioning, in lesser detail, the earlier operas (*Die Feen*, *Das Liebesverbot* and *Rienzi*), the prose sketches for *Die Meistersinger* (1845), *Friedrich I.* (1846–9), *Jesus von Nazareth* (1849) and *Wieland der Schmied* (1850), and the Nibelung project, which was even then undergoing transformation from a single drama to a tetralogy.

However, the opening paragraph of *Eine Mitteilung* betrays a hidden agenda. The need had arisen, Wagner suggests there, to account for the contradiction between the 'character and form' of the Romantic operas and the theoretical principles laid down in the recently published essay *Oper und Drama*. Wagner's approach to operatic composition was undergoing a critical change at this time, and *Eine Mitteilung* can be seen, on one level, as an attempt to make the three earlier operas conform to the aesthetic criteria propounded in *Oper und Drama*. Thus all three are characterized as incipient through-composed music dramas, with the entire score of the *Holländer* germinating from the 'thematic seed' planted in Senta's Ballad.

More problematic is the philosophical underpinning of these works, in particular of *Lohengrin*. Wagner's exegesis of what we would now call the gender relations of *Lohengrin* – his empathy with Elsa as the unconscious, implicitly loving female principle capable of redeeming conscious, egoistic man – owes a good deal to both Feuerbach and the revolutionary, *völkisch* ideals which were ostensibly not embraced by the composer until the late 1840s. It should be pointed out, however, that although the text of *Lohengrin* was completed in November 1845, the work as a whole took a further two or three years to finish; that Feuerbachian/revolutionary ideals were in the air earlier in the decade too; and that Wagner's retrospective interpretation of his work is not necessarily invalidated by the chronology, since every great work of art contains more than its creator could consciously intend.

One of the purposes behind Wagner's chief autobiographical project, *Mein Leben*, was similarly to 'refute all the distortions & calumnies' supposedly circulating about him. However, in attempting to provide a corrective to the many scurrilous reports that had indeed been launched even before his controversial relationship with King Ludwig II, Wagner succumbed all too readily to the temptation prevalent among autobiographers to paint an idealized picture of their lives. Thus Wagner's predisposition to place himself in a line of succession that ran through Aeschylus, Shakespeare, Goethe and Beethoven caused him to misrepresent, either consciously or unconsciously, certain key experiences. The implausibility of it being Schröder-Devrient's Leonore that made such an indelible impression on the 16-year-old composer (as opposed to her Romeo in

23

Bellini's *I Capuleti e i Montecchi*) has been well documented, as has the real inspiration for Wagner's *Faust Ouvertüre*. Other examples of mythologization – concerning the geneses of *Der fliegende Holländer*, *Das Rheingold* and *Parsifal* – have been noted above.

In spite of – or perhaps in the light of – such distortions, *Mein Leben* remains an invaluable testimony to the aspirations and achievements of a composer determined to place himself at the centre of the world stage. The period covered by the autobiography is 1813 (Wagner's birth) to 1864 (his 'rescue' by Ludwig II). In response to a request from the king, Wagner began, on 17 July 1865, to dictate it to Cosima, using notes from his 'Red Pocketbook'. The dictation occupied some 15 years (albeit with interruptions), being completed on 25 July 1880. The work was divided into four volumes, of which the first three were published by G.A. Bonfantini of Basle between 1870 and 1875. Volume 4 was published by Theodor Burger of Bayreuth in 1880. Only 15 copies of the first volume were ordered, and 18 of each of the remaining volumes. They were sent to close friends and associates but recalled by Cosima after Wagner's death. An extra copy of the first three volumes had, however, been made by Bonfantini for himself, and these were subsequently acquired (in 1892) by the collector Mary Burrell. *Mein Leben* finally entered the public domain with the edition of 1911, which was severely compromised by numerous printing errors (for which Cosima's handwriting was partly responsible) and by the suppression or falsifying of some 17 passages, largely concerning people still alive at the time. Martin Gregor-Dellin's 'first authentic edition' (A 1963) was a marked improvement, though a fully annotated, critical edition is still awaited.

7. DRAMATIC WORKS

Nothing more vividly demonstrates the multiplicity of genres available to composers of opera in the first decades of the 19th century than the stylistic variety of Wagner's first three operas, *Die Feen*, *Das Liebesverbot* and *Rienzi*. In *Die Feen* the model was German Romantic opera, especially as developed by Weber and Marschner: the supernatural subject matter, the enhanced role of the orchestra and the shift away from static, closed forms towards organic growth are all evident, to at least some degree. Acts 2 and 3 each contain a fine scene and aria, the latter, depicting the mental derangement of Arindal, a complex in which recitative, arioso and aria are juxtaposed. One of the work's most inventive numbers, the comic duet for Drolla and Gernot in Act 2, is untypical in its *opera buffa*-style patter. *Die Feen* is marked by the return of a few characteristic melodic ideas, but scarcely with a persistence such as to merit the term 'leitmotif'.

Das Liebesverbot has a handful of recurring motifs, of which the most prominent is that associated with Friedrich's ban on love; it occasionally returns to make an ironic comment on the dramatic situation, as when Friedrich himself is tempted by passion (Act 1 finale). Wagner's models in the case of *Das Liebesverbot* were Italian and French opera, especially Bellini and Auber; vestiges remain of the *opéra comique* convention of spoken dialogue. German influences should not, however, be overlooked. That Wagner was absorbed at this period in the works of, particularly, Marschner is evident, and there are direct reminiscences of Beethoven's *Fidelio*, including an imitation of Leonore's 'Töt' erst sein Weib!' at the climax of the trial scene ('Erst hört noch mich').

With *Rienzi* Wagner turned his attention to grand opera, his explicit intention being to gain a popular success at the Opéra in Paris. Meyerbeer, with his spectacular large-scale effects, was naturally a primary model, but the influence of Spontini, Auber and Halévy, all of whom Wagner admired, is also evident. In his desire to 'outdo all previous examples' with the sumptuousness of his own grand opera, Wagner imposed a grandiosity of scale on material scarcely able to support it. The powerful but empty rhetoric that results has been seen as both a reflection of the extravagant pomp with which the historical Rienzi surrounded himself, and as an emblem of totalitarianism inherent in the work. Wagner's resumption of work on *Rienzi* after his move from Riga to Paris coincided with his growing dissatisfaction with the discrete number form of conventional opera. Acts 3 to 5 begin to embody the principles of unified poetry and music enunciated in such Paris essays and novellas as *Eine Pilgerfahrt zu Beethoven* (1840); the change is subtle, but is seen in a more expressive, more poetically aware use of recitative that foreshadows the arioso of the mature style, and in the occasional use of the orchestra to comment independently on the action.

Wagner's intention, in *Der fliegende Holländer*, to sweep away the 'tiresome operatic accessories' altogether was not completely realized, but there is a further shift towards the kind of organic continuity that was already evident in such German Romantic scores as Weber's *Euryanthe* (1822–3) and that was to distinguish the mature Wagnerian music drama. Recitative is still present in the score of the *Holländer* and referred to as such. Arias, duets, trios and choruses are also present, but such divisions as, for example, 'scene, duet and chorus' (Daland and the Dutchman, Act 1) have suggested the designation 'scene opera' in preference to 'number opera'. In the treatment of the duets for Erik and Senta and for the Dutchman and Senta (both Act 2) there are already signs of the greater precedence to be accorded the setting of words, though quadratic phrase structure (i.e. in regular multiples of two or four bars) is still the norm. As for ensembles, the Sailors' Chorus at the end of Act 1 and the Spinning Chorus in Act 2, despite their clever linking by the orchestra's development of a dotted figure common to both, are not closely integrated into the work's structure; the choruses of the Norwegian and Dutch crews in Act 3, on the other hand, do serve a more dramatic function in their vying for supremacy. Significantly, the fidelity to, and departure from, conventional operatic norms is related to the two strikingly contrasted worlds of the *Holländer*: the exterior world of reality to which belong Daland, Erik, the spinning girls and the sailors, and the interior world of the imagination inhabited by Senta and the Dutchman. Erik's two arias, for example, represent the most old-fashioned writing in the work, while the Dutchman's Act 1 monologue frequently manages to break free from the constraints of regular periodic structure.

A similar dualism is evident in *Tannhäuser*, where traditional operatic structures are associated with the sphere of the reactionary Wartburg court, while a more progressive style is associated with the Venusberg. To the former belong, for example, the more or less self-contained arias of the song contest, Elisabeth's two set-piece arias, her conventional duet with Tannhäuser, and Wolfram's celebrated aria 'O du mein holder Abendstern', highly conservative in its regular eight-bar periods and tonal scheme. Venus's music, by contrast, is more radically advanced: her contributions to the duet with Tannhäuser (Act 1) continually breach the constraints of quadratic periods (notably contrasting with Tannhäuser's own more formal utterances), and both that scene and the preceding Bacchanal are progressive in their harmonic vocabulary and rhythmic structure – especially in the Paris version. The most advanced writing in *Tannhäuser*, however, occurs in the Rome Narration (Act 3), where the expressive demands of the text are satisfied by a flexible form of dramatic recitative or arioso responsive to verbal nuance; the orchestra also assumes a major illustrative role here, bearing the burden of the dramatic argument. Another primary dualism present in *Tannhäuser* (related to that of Venusberg and Wartburg) is the traditional struggle between sensuality and spirituality – a dualism reflected in an 'associative' use of tonality. E major is associated with the Venusberg, and E♭ with the pilgrims, holy love and salvation. Thus Wolfram's E♭ hymn to 'noble love' (Act 2) is abruptly interrupted by the delayed fourth verse of Tannhäuser's Hymn to Venus in E. Similarly, the Rome Narration reaches E♭ as Tannhäuser recounts how he stood before the Pope; after a series of modulations the enticements of the Venusberg reappear in E, but the final triumphant return to E♭ confirms Tannhäuser's salvation.

The 'associative' use of tonality is also evident in *Lohengrin*. Lohengrin himself and the sphere of the Grail are represented by A major, Elsa with A♭ major (and minor), while Ortrud and her magical powers are associated with F♯ minor (the relative minor of Lohengrin's tonality), and the King's trumpeters on stage with C major. In the second and third scenes of Act 1, the tonalities of Lohengrin and Elsa, a semitone apart, are deployed skilfully to symbolic and expressive effect. *Lohengrin*, like the *Holländer* and *Tannhäuser*, contains various motifs associated with characters or concepts, but in general (the motif of the Forbidden Question is an exception) these do not conform to the strict prescriptions to be laid down in *Oper und Drama*; they also tend to be fully rounded themes rather than pithy ideas capable of infinite transformation, and do not therefore serve the vital structural function of the leitmotifs in the *Ring*. For all that *Lohengrin* marks a stylistic advance over the earlier operas, it fails to fulfil several criteria of the fully fledged music drama. Vestiges of grand opera are still present in the use of diablerie, spectacle and crowd scenes, with minster, organ, fanfares and bridal procession. Traces of old-fashioned number form are still evident, but recitatives, arias, duets and choruses (even those numbers, such as Elsa's Dream or Lohengrin's narration, which have become celebrated as independent set pieces) are in fact carefully integrated into the musical fabric. The two latter pieces, at least after their conventional openings, display a greater propensity for irregular phrase structures than most numbers in *Lohengrin*. The quadratic phrase patterns that dominate the work, together with the virtual absence of triple time, impart a uniformity of rhythmic impulse that may be perceived as ponderousness.

Several fundamental changes characterize the musical language of the *Ring*, as Wagner began, in *Das Rheingold*, to implement the principles enunciated in the theoretical essays of 1849–51. In the first place, regular phrase patterns give way to fluid arioso structures in which the text is projected in a vocal line that faithfully reflects its verbal accentuations, poetic meaning and emotional content. On occasion in *Rheingold*, the rigorous attempt to match poetic shape with musical phrase results in pedestrian melodic ideas. But in *Walküre* the musico-poetic synthesis is found at its most ingenious, interesting melodic lines registering the finer nuances of the text with no unnatural word stresses. The Forging Song in Act 1 of *Siegfried* gives notice of a shift towards musical predominance, while Act 3 of *Siegfried* and *Götterdämmerung*, for all the fine examples of scrupulous matching of words and music, exhibit a tendency towards quick-fire exchanges, as found in *Die Meistersinger* but modified in accordance with the elevated tone of the tetralogy.

Hand in hand with this evolution of musico-poetic synthesis go developments in formal structure and in the use of leitmotif. The excessively rigid symmetries of Lorenz's analyses (an over-reaction to charges of formlessness in Wagner's music) have now been rejected, or rather radically modified to take account also of such elements as period and phrase structure, orchestration and tempo. Lorenz's arch-(*ABA*) and *Bar*-(*AAB*) forms are indeed present in Wagner, but like the other traditional forms of strophic song, rondo and variation, they are constantly adapted, often in midstream, creating new, hybrid forms notable for their complexity and ambiguity.

The leitmotif (though never actually called that by Wagner) takes on a structural role in the *Ring*, whereas, in *Lohengrin*, its function was purely dramatic. As Wagner suggested in his 1879 essay *Über die Anwendung der Musik auf das Drama*, motivic transformation provides a key to the analysis of his music dramas; but he went on to say that his transformations were generated according to dramatic imperatives and as such would be incomprehensible in a symphonic structure. It is the dramatic origination of the motifs that is responsible for their frequent association with specific tonalities. The Tarnhelm motif, for example, is associated with G♯ minor and that of the Curse with B minor. Modulatory passages are common in which the primary tonality of an important motif is engineered. Sometimes, too, the tonality in question becomes the determining key of a whole section or structural unit (the return of B minor for the Curse motif in Scene 4 of *Rheingold*, as Fasolt is murdered by Fafner, is an example of this).

The deployment of motifs in the *Ring* underwent a change during the course of composition. In *Rheingold* the identification of motifs with specific objects or ideas is at its most unambiguous. In *Walküre* and the first two acts of *Siegfried*, motivic representation is still made according to reasonably strict musico-poetic criteria, but without quite the literal-mindedness of *Rheingold*. In Act 3 of *Siegfried* and *Götterdämmerung*, however, written after the long break in composition, the motifs frequently aspire to an independent life of their own. They are combined in such profusion and with such contrapuntal virtuosity that it is clear that the principles of *Oper und Drama* are no longer being strictly adhered to. In *Rheingold* the thematic transformations that take place in the passages linking the scenes are not typical of the work; the score of *Götterdämmerung*, however, is characterized by congeries of motifs drawn on for a brief thematic development.

Just as certain leitmotifs are associated with specific tonalities, so groups of characters (though, unlike the earlier operas, not individual characters) are also identified with particular keys: the Valkyries with B minor, the Nibelungs with B♭ minor. The entire Nibelheim Scene (Scene 3) of *Rheingold*, for example, is dominated by B♭ minor, which even interrupts Loge's A major music as Alberich asserts himself. The B♭ minor of the Nibelheim Scene is framed by the D♭ major in which Scene 2 begins and Scene 4 ends. The relative key, contrasting but intimately connected, denotes the relationship of Wotan (Licht-Alberich) to Alberich. If the first scene of *Rheingold* is excluded (since it is in the nature of a prelude, outside the main action and its time zone), the tetralogy both begins and ends in D♭ major; it should not be regarded as the chief tonality to which all others are related, but it does provide a framework of sorts, and at the end affords a sense of homecoming. *Rheingold* was originally conceived by Wagner as a drama in three acts with a prelude, a structure which replicates not only that of *Götterdämmerung* (three acts and a prologue) but also that of the *Ring* as a whole.

The tendency towards the non-specificity of leitmotifs in the course of the *Ring* is continued in *Tristan und Isolde*. Aptly for a work dealing in metaphysical abstractions, motifs are not used in the latter to symbolize swords and spears; nor can they generally be confined to a single concept (the motifs associated with 'death' and 'day' are exceptions). The elusiveness of the motifs and their associations is reflected in their propensity for interrelation by means of thematic transformation. And if the abstract nature of the motifs in *Tristan* enhances their flexibility, making them more conducive to 'symphonic' development, they are also more closely integrated into the harmonic structure of the work: the melodic line of the motif associated with the words 'Todgeweihtes Haupt!; Todgeweihtes Herz!' is a product of the chromatic progression A♭–A, not vice versa.

The elevation of motivic interplay to an abstract level in *Tristan* is accompanied by a further shift in the balance of music and text towards the former. There are still many examples of musico-poetic synthesis that conform to *Oper und Drama* principles, but there is also an increased tendency towards vowel extension, melisma, and overlapping and simultaneous declamation of the singers, not to mention the opulent orchestration with triple wind – all of which conspire to reduce the clarity with which the text is projected. The extended vowels of Brangäne's Watchsong, for example, render her words virtually inaudible; the text is not irrelevant, but has been absorbed into the music to create an intensified line that is then reintegrated into the orchestral fabric.

The temporal values of society represented by Marke and Melot, and the earthly humanity of Kurwenal, are often matched by foursquare diatonicism. Conversely, the neurotic self-absorption of Tristan and Isolde and their unassuageable yearning are reflected in the work's prevailing mode of chromaticism; suspensions, unresolved dissonances and sequential variation are ubiquitous and chromatically heightened. Every element, poetical and musical, is geared to the generation and intensification of tension – the tension of promised but evaded fulfilment.

The vocal line undergoes a further development in *Die Meistersinger*. For much of the time it is little more than recitative, but its bareness is counteracted by the orchestra's richness of detail; the orchestra is by now firmly established as the chief commentator on the dramatic action. The improvisatory nature of the musical texture corresponds to the principle that Wagner was to codify in *Über die Bestimmung der Oper* (1871), whereby the improvisatory element in acting was to be harnessed to the essential improvisatory ingredient in musical composition, resulting in a 'fixed improvisation'.

The subject matter of the music drama – the creation of a mastersong – might seem to lend weight to Lorenz's formal analysis in terms of *Bar*-form. But this would be to reckon without the more flexible, more sophisticated structures that Wagner had been developing throughout his career, and without the element of parody that is central to the work (Voss in Csampai and Holland, N 1981). Aspects of *Bar*-form are indeed present but often in an ironic context: the variation entailed in the *AAB* structure of 'Am stillen Herd', for example, is absurdly florid.

A similar distancing tendency is at work in Wagner's persistent use in *Die Meistersinger* of such traditional forms as set-piece arias, ensembles and choruses; all three acts end with a massed finale worthy of grand opera. The forms of Walther's arias or of Beckmesser's Serenade tell us as much about the characters and their dramatic predicament as the notes themselves. The irregular phrase lengths, false accentuations and disorderly progress of the Serenade depict Beckmesser's agitation and artistic sterility, and should not be regarded as symptomatic of an 'advanced' musical style (unlike the Act 3 'pantomime' in Hans Sachs's study, which does look to the future in its graphic musical pictorialism).

Old and new are fused also in the musical language: the work's predominant diatonicism has an archaic tendency, largely as a result of the penchant for secondary triads with their modal flavour. If this challenge to the traditional tonic-dominant hierarchy is a musical metaphor for *Die Meistersinger*'s nostalgic retrospection, it is at the same time a means of rejuvenating tonality.

In *Parsifal* Wagner the librettist supplied Wagner the composer with some of his freest verse, ranging from sonorous, measured lines to violently expressive ones. The vocal lines which resulted similarly range from more or less melodic arioso (though often the primary idea is in the orchestra and the vocal line functions rather as counterpoint) to a form of recitative-like declamation (for example in Gurnemanz's Act 1 narration). There are leitmotifs which can be identified with objects or concepts, such as the Spear, the Last Supper or the Grail, but the associations are not rigidly consistent: as in *Tristan*, the function of the motifs is less representational than to provide raw material for 'symphonic' development.

Again as in *Tristan* and *Die Meistersinger*, the modes of chromaticism and diatonicism are counterposed, but whereas in those two works the signification was relatively clear, in *Parsifal* the relationship of the two is more equivocal. The realms of the Grail and of Klingsor are associated with diatonicism and chromaticism respectively, but between these two poles are many cross-currents: Amfortas's suffering, for example, conforms exclusively to neither category, confirming that his experience, while ultimately the catalyst for the redemptive process, is tainted by depravity. The propensity for tonal dissolution, in *Parsifal*, for diatonicism to yield to chromaticism, is a potent metaphor for the theme of spiritual degeneration. Tritones, augmented triads and median tonal relationships, which all undermine the tonic-dominant hierarchy, contribute to the uncertain nature of a tonal continuum that veers between diatonicism and chromaticism, stable and unstable tonality. Ambiguity also surrounds the polarity of A♭ major and D (major and minor), which are evidently not to be viewed as irreconcilably opposing forces but as complementary spheres to be brought into resolution. The final stage in that process takes place at the setting of Parsifal's last words, 'Enthüllet den Gral', which effects a modulation from D major to the A♭ with which the work unequivocally concludes.

8. NON-DRAMATIC AND INCOMPLETE WORKS

ORCHESTRAL

Like all composers of his era, Wagner grew up in the shadow of Beethoven and the Classical symphonic tradition. His obsession with Beethoven, revealed both in the autobiographical writings and in fictional stories such as the novella *Eine Pilgerfahrt zu Beethoven*, reflected a perceived need to confront that tradition, acknowledging the legacy of Beethoven and at the same time staking a claim as his natural successor.

The music drama was, of course, the genre evolved by Wagner as the ideal vehicle for reconciling symphonic principles with a literary and philosophical content. Before arriving at that solution, he made various attempts to address the problem in purely orchestral terms, and at different periods in his life he gave serious consideration to the possibility of symphonic composition. Some nine or ten orchestral pieces, mostly overtures (of which half have not survived), were conceived by Wagner between 1830 and 1832, the student years during which he took composition lessons from C.T. Weinlig. The first significant landmark, however, was the Symphony in C major of 1832, an impressively constructed work, full of Beethovenian gestures yet strongly individual in its dramatic impulse and colouring. Of a second symphony, in E major, dating from 1834, only the first movement – influenced by Beethoven's Pastoral Symphony and the overtures of Weber – was completed. The autograph is lost, but a score in the hand of Mottl resurfaced in Munich in the late 1980s. Mendelssohn was the undoubted influence in the overture to Apel's play *Columbus* (1834–5), while the self-parodying attempts to outstrip Beethoven in the *Rule Britannia* Overture (1837) have an unintentionally comic effect in performance. The chief inspiration for the *Faust-Ouvertüre* (1839–40, revised 1855) came, *pace* Wagner's account in *Mein Leben*, probably not from Beethoven's Ninth Symphony (though there are some undoubted similarities), but from Berlioz's *Roméo et Juliette*, which impressed Wagner at the time as a potential solution to the problem of reconciling a literary impulse with abstract symphonic form.

Beethoven's Ninth, on the other hand, probably was a major factor in the reawakening of Wagner's symphonic ambitions in 1846–7, from which period sketches exist for at least two symphonies. At this time Wagner was engaged in the composition of *Lohengrin* in Dresden, but he was also making assiduous preparations for the performance of the Ninth at the traditional Palm Sunday concert in the old opera house in the same city. There seems little doubt that his close study of the work stimulated this brief burst of symphonic inspiration.

From Wagner's maturity date three occasional marches. The *Huldigungsmarsch* was composed to celebrate the birthday of Ludwig II on 25 August 1864. The original version was for military band; an orchestral arrangement was made in part by the composer and in part by Joachim Raff. The *Kaisermarsch* of 1871 pandered to the mood of militant nationalism following the proclamation of the Second Reich and the German victory in the Franco-Prussian war. This piece too was originally scored for a military band, but subsequently arranged, in this case by the composer himself, for a full orchestra. An optional jingoistic 'people's chorus' was also added later. The *Grosser Festmarsch* ('Centennial March') was composed in 1876 to a commission to celebrate the hundredth anniversary of the American Declaration of Independence.

In marked contrast, the *Siegfried Idyll* is one of Wagner's most intimate works, conceived as it was as a birthday present for Cosima in 1870 and as a retrospective celebration of the birth of their son Siegfried and of the composition of Act 3 of *Siegfried*, both the previous year. The first performance of the *Idyll* took place on the staircase at Tribschen, outside Cosima's bedroom, and the modest forces involved (probably 15 players rather than the oft-cited 13) were doubtless, in part, the result of logistical considerations. Certainly, in spite of the intimate associations of the work for the composer and his wife, Wagner intended it to be performed by a rather larger ensemble: for a private performance in Mannheim in 1871 he requested at least 23 strings rather than the original eight, while in 1874 he was planning an arrangement for 'a large orchestra'. The phrase 'symphonic birthday greeting' in the title-page inscription in the autograph, taken together with the structure of the work (a broadly based, modified sonata form), further confirms the relevance of the *Idyll* to Wagner's symphonic ambitions.

That such ambitions had not been relinquished even in the last years of his life is evident from the plans (none of which was realized) to compose overtures and symphonies. The former were conceived, between January 1874 and February 1875, as a set of large-scale orchestral overtures with programmatic titles, such as 'Lohengrin's Ocean Voyage' (later 'Lohengrin's Journey') and 'Tristan the Hero'. The symphonies which Wagner planned and sketched between autumn 1877 and his death in February 1883 were intended as a continuation of the Beethovenian tradition, though they were to be single-movement structures. As for the symphonic process itself, Wagner's comments (reported by Cosima in various diary entries) are somewhat contradictory. Originally he proposed to call his pieces 'symphonic dialogues' because they would consist of theme and countertheme in conversation; later, however, he suggested that ideas should emerge out of one another – a process more akin to thematic metamorphosis.

CHORAL

Between 1834 and 1836 Wagner was attached to a theatrical troupe in Magdeburg. The troupe's stage director, Wilhelm Schmale, wrote a festival play to celebrate the new year, and Wagner was required, in a short space of time, to contribute incidental music. The five numbers he wrote were an overture (incorporating music from the slow movement of the C major Symphony), choruses and 'allegorical music'. In 1837, during his period in Riga, Wagner was commissioned to write a *Volks-Hymne* (national anthem) for the birthday celebrations of Tsar Nicholas. Giving the music 'as despotic and patriarchal a colouring as possible', he achieved a popular success that was performed on the same day in subsequent years.

Demonstrating further a pragmatic but impressive stylistic flexibility in these early years, the chorus 'Descendons gaiment la courtille' was written to be interpolated in the two-scene vaudeville *La descente de la courtille*, which had its first performance at the Théâtre des Variétés in Paris on 20 January 1841. The light French style, popularized subsequently by Offenbachian operetta, could hardly be more alien to the weighty Teutonic idiom soon to be embraced by Wagner.

Four choral pieces date from Wagner's years as Kapellmeister in Dresden. *Der Tag erscheint* for male chorus (1843) was composed for the unveiling of a memorial to King Friedrich August I of Saxony. The chorus was sung *a cappella* on that occasion, but Wagner also made a version, probably at about the same time, for male chorus and brass instruments. The most substantial work of the group is *Das Liebesmahl der Apostel* (1843), a 'Biblical scene' on the subject of the first Pentecost, written for a gala performance given by all the male choral societies in Saxony. At the first performance, in the Dresden Frauenkirche, there were some 1200 singers and 100 orchestral players. The male chorus *Gruss seiner Treuen an Friedrich August den Geliebten* (1844) was composed to celebrate the return of King Friedrich August II of Saxony from England. Its refrain combines two melodic ideas shortly to be used in Act 2 of *Tannhäuser*. Another male chorus, *An Webers Grabe* (1844), was written for the occasion of the reinterment of Weber's remains in Dresden. A torchlit procession on 14 December 1844 was accompanied by Wagner's *Trauermusik* (based on three themes from *Euryanthe*) for wind band (including 20 clarinets, 10 bassoons and 14 horns) and muffled drums; on the following morning, by the side of the grave in the Friedrichstadt cemetery, Wagner gave an oration and conducted his chorus.

With the exception of the nine-bar *Wahlspruch für die deutsche Feuerwehr* ('Motto for the German Fire Brigade') of 1869, Wagner wrote no more choral pieces until the small group, all for children's voices, celebrating marital bliss (and more specifically Cosima's birthdays), dating from the last decade. The *Kinder-Katechismus* (1873), for which Wagner's verse was in question-and-answer form, exists in two versions, the second with an accompaniment for a small orchestra. The eight-bar chorus *Willkommen in Wahnfried, du heil'ger Christ* (1877) was performed in Wahnfried for Cosima by the children, as was *Ihr Kinder, geschwinde, geschwinde* three years later.

CHAMBER

An early string quartet in D major (1829) has not survived, and the so-called 'Starnberg Quartet', supposedly dating from the 1860s, has been shown to be a mythical creation (Voss, N 1977, and Millington, I 1992), despite a putative 'reconstruction' by Gerald Abraham published in 1947. The Adagio for clarinet and string quintet, formerly attributed to Wagner, is in fact by Heinrich Joseph Baermann, belonging to his Clarinet Quintet, op.23.

SOLO VOICE AND ORCHESTRA

The only surviving works in this category are a series of interpolations for operas by other composers, all dating from Wagner's prentice years. 'Doch jetzt wohin ich blicke', an effective display piece, was a new allegro ending for Aubry's aria 'Wie ein schöner Frühlingsmorgen' in Marschner's *Der Vampyr*, which Wagner was responsible for rehearsing in Würzburg (1833). He opened his first season as music director of the theatre in Riga (1837) with Carl Blum's comic opera *Mary, Max und Michel*, for which he composed an extra bass aria entitled 'Sanfte Wehmut will sich regen'. Another bass aria, composed for insertion in Joseph Weigl's 'lyrical opera' *Die Schweizerfamilie*, was lost until 1994, while 'Norma il predisse, O Druidi' was intended to be sung by the celebrated bass Luigi Lablache (who politely declined) in Bellini's *Norma*.

SOLO VOICE AND PIANO

Among Wagner's earliest compositions is a set of seven pieces for either solo voice or chorus (or both) and piano for inclusion in a performance of Goethe's *Faust* (1831). More significant is the group of songs Wagner wrote between 1838 and 1840, in the hope of making his reputation in Paris. The idea that celebrated singers should include these songs in their concerts came to nothing, however. *Extase*, *La tombe dit à la rose* and *Attente* (the first two of which exist only in fragmentary form) were all settings of poems by Victor Hugo. *Dors mon enfant* and *Mignonne*, together with *Attente*, were published in Paris by Durand, Schoenewerk et Cie in 1870. *Tout n'est qu'images fugitives* is a setting of a poem enti-tled *Soupir* by Jean Reboul, while *Les deux grenadiers* sets a French translation of the poem by Heine, more famously set by Schumann. The song with the grandest operatic gestures of all is *Adieux de Marie Stuart*, evoking the tearful farewell to France of Mary Queen of Scots. Various of the above songs are included in recitals from time to time, but their fame is dwarfed by that of the *Wesendonck Lieder*, a set of five songs to texts by Mathilde Wesendonck (1857–8). Two of the songs were designated by Wagner 'studies for *Tristan and Isolde*': *Im Treibhaus*, which antici-pates the bleak prelude to Act 3, and *Träume*, which looks forward to the Act 2 duet. As a birthday present for Mathilde, Wagner also arranged *Träume* for solo violin and chamber orchestra, and conducted it at the Wesendoncks' villa in Zürich on 23 December 1857. The orchestral version of the other four songs gen-erally performed today is by Felix Mottl, though Henze also made a version of the complete set – a more radical but sensitive rescoring – in 1976.

PIANO

Wagner's works for piano fall into two groups: those dating from his student years and those written for and dedicated to particular individuals at various points in his life. The works in the first group – disregarding a pair of lost sonatas from 1829 – were composed in Leipzig in 1831 and 1832. The primary influence in the sonatas in B♭ and A is Beethoven, but the more quirkily indi-vidual Fantasia in F♯ minor also betrays Wagner's fascination at that time with Bellinian bel canto.

The earliest work in the second group was the Albumblatt in E major (the title 'Lied ohne Worte' was added on its first publication in 1911), apparently written for Ernst Benedikt Kietz in 1840. Further Albumblätter were composed for Princess Pauline Metternich (1861), Countess Pourtalès ('Ankunft bei den schwarzen Schwänen', also 1861) and Betty Schott (1875). Wagner's most sub-stantial work for piano, however, is the sonata for Mathilde Wesendonck (*Sonate für das Album von Frau MW*), a comparatively rare example in the 19th century of a single sonata-form movement (as opposed to the Lisztian model of several movements integrated into one).

PROJECTED AND UNFINISHED DRAMATIC WORKS

The five-act tragedy *Leubald* (1826–8), dating from Wagner's adolescence, was the earliest of his ambitious dramatic schemes, drawing, as he later reported in

Mein Leben, on *Hamlet*, *Macbeth* and *King Lear*, as well as Goethe's *Götz von Berlichingen*. He planned incidental music for it in the style of Beethoven's *Egmont*, but if any was written, it has not survived.

Die Hochzeit (1832–3) was specifically conceived as an opera, but the poem is lost, and of the music only an introduction, chorus and septet were written. The prose scenario for *Die hohe Braut, oder Bianca und Giuseppe*, a grand opera in four or five acts, was probably sketched by Wagner in Königsberg in 1836. He subsequently sent it to Scribe in Paris, in the hope that the librettist might develop it into a text which Wagner could then be commissioned to set to music for the Opéra. *Die hohe Braut* was eventually elaborated into a libretto, however, by Wagner himself in Dresden, in 1842, and set to music by J.B. Kittl.

Männerlist grösser als Frauenlist, oder Die glückliche Bärenfamilie ('Man's Cunning Greater than Woman's, or The Happy Bear Family', ?1838), based on a story from *The Thousand and One Nights*, was intended as a comic opera, in the form of a Singspiel, with prose dialogue and individual numbers, for three of which sketches survive. *Die Sarazenin* ('The Saracen Woman'), a projected five-act opera, on the subject of the Hohenstaufen prince Manfred, son of Friedrich II, and a mysterious Saracen prophetess, Fatima, was conceived almost certainly in Paris, late in 1841. Wagner subsequently elaborated his draft in Dresden, in 1843, but proceeded no further, and wrote no music for it. *Die Bergwerke zu Falun* ('The Mines of Falun', 1842), based on a story by E.T.A. Hoffmann, was another aborted project also dating from Wagner's Paris years. The years surrounding the Dresden uprisings of 1848–9 produced four different attempts to find a satisfactory vehicle for ideas that achieved final form in the *Ring*: the historical subject of Friedrich I (the 12th-century emperor Friedrich Barbarossa) was abandoned (though not quite as readily as Wagner later suggested) in favour of the greater potential afforded by the Nibelung myth, while a three-act drama on the subject of Achilles, with its themes of a free hero and of the gods yielding to humanity, the five-act *Jesus von Nazareth*, with its advocacy of a new religion of humanity, and the 'heroic opera' *Wieland der Schmied* were similarly all superseded by the *Ring*. The Buddhist subject matter of *Die Sieger* ('The Victors'), dealing with the conflict between passion and chastity, preoccupied Wagner from the mid-1850s until the end of his life, but again the theme was treated definitively in another work, *Parsifal*.

Only prose sketches exist for the drama *Luthers Hochzeit* (1868), treating one of the decisive acts of the Reformation – Luther's rejection of his priestly celibacy and his marriage to Catharina von Bora – and Wagner appears not to have attempted to compose any music; ten years later he considered writing a prose play on the subject. *Eine Kapitulation* (1870), described as a 'comedy in the antique style', was a heavy-handed farce in somewhat dubious taste, set in Paris at the time of the siege in that city. Wagner did not set the text himself, but he may have tinkered with the setting undertaken by Hans Richter, which has not survived (possibly destroyed by Richter himself).

9. ORCHESTRATION

A paradox lies at the heart of Wagner's orchestration. As his compositional ambitions developed through the three early operas, the trio of German Romantic operas and the *Ring* tetralogy, culminating in the final three master-pieces, so the tonal resources of the existing orchestra were expanded. Yet larger forces did not – contrary to the impression given by contemporary caricatures – simply lead to greater volume and cruder effects. On the contrary, to compare the exuberant tambourines and castanets of *Das Liebesverbot*, or the bombastic, massive rhetoric of *Rienzi*, with the rich, velvety textures of the *Ring* or the refined sonorities of *Parsifal*, famously described by Debussy as 'illuminated as from behind', is to realize just how central the art of orchestration was to Wagner's project.

On one level, this development reflects Wagner's own progress towards mastery. Again, one may compare the overwrought triangle part in the early concert overture *Rule Britannia* with the single stroke of the instrument in the closing bars of Act 2 of *Siegfried* – praised by Strauss as a 'wise application of the triangle'. Similarly, the insistent cymbals of *Das Liebesverbot*, the massed brass of *Rienzi* or the extravagant six trumpets of the early *Columbus* Overture may be compared with the magical *pianissimo* brushing of the cymbals at the start of the long final descent in the *Lohengrin* prelude, or the delicate touches on a solo trumpet in the second stanza of Elsa's Dream (Act 1 of the same opera).

On another level, the increased sophistication of Wagner's scoring accords with developments in the 19th century generally. The beginning of the century heralded the liberation of woodwind and brass instruments, whose sonorities, both solo and in combination, now made more distinctive contributions to the orchestral texture. In opera, more specifically, such composers as Spontini and Weber were employing these timbres imaginatively, adding new colours to the tonal palette; such innovations were soon extended by Berlioz and Meyerbeer as well as Wagner.

The demands of narrative and characterization in opera fuelled these develop-ments, the Wagnerian technique of leitmotif underlining further the association between particular timbres and characters, objects, concepts or emotions. In *Lohengrin*, according to Liszt, the work's first conductor, each of the elements has its own distinctive colouring: strings for the Holy Grail, wind for Elsa, brass for Heinrich. Richard Strauss also admired *Lohengrin*, in particular for Wagner's deployment of the *dritte Bläser* – i.e. the addition of the cor anglais to the two oboes, and the bass clarinet to the two clarinets, to form homogeneous and potentially autonomous choruses alongside the three flutes and three bassoons.

In accordance with the general trend in the 19th century, Wagner's mature orchestra was notable for its considerable reinforcement of strings in relation to woodwind. For the *Ring* he asked for 16 first violins, 16 seconds, 12 violas, 12 cellos and 8 double basses. Admittedly he called also for quadruple woodwind in the *Ring*, as in *Parsifal*, though only triple for *Tristan*, and double (plus piccolo/third flute) for *Die Meistersinger*. The ensuing carpet of string sound is a characteristic feature of Wagner's scores, but there are also countless examples of subtle, delicate effects obtained in a variety of ways.

Expanding the tonal resources of the orchestra involved both the redeployment of existing instruments and experimentation with new ones. In the first category belong the trombones. If trombones were becoming standard in opera house orchestras throughout Europe in the 19th century, then it was Wagner above all who gave them an independent voice. Their enunciations of the striding Spear motif, or that of the baleful Curse, in the *Ring* proclaimed a new freedom that made possible even more radical innovations in subsequent eras. Perhaps the most significant of the 'new' instruments were the 'Wagner tubas'. Called tenor and bass tubas in the score, they are generally blown, with horn mouthpieces, by a quartet of horn players, and were intended to bridge the gap between horns and trombones. Wagner's 'invention' of these instruments owed much to the experiments of Adolphe Sax and others, just as the bass trumpet and contrabass trombone he had constructed for the *Ring* also drew on military band precedents. Wagner called for an alto oboe to be specially constructed for the *Ring* and *Parsifal*, but the instrument failed to establish itself permanently. The bass clarinet was not a Wagnerian invention, but it was exploited as a melodic instrument in *Tristan* and as a useful bass to the woodwind choir elsewhere.

Other special instruments used by Wagner include the 18 anvils in the *Ring*; the cow horns in *Die Walküre*, *Götterdämmerung* and *Die Meistersinger*; the wind machine in *Der fliegende Holländer*; and the Grail bells which are not the least of the many problematic issues in *Parsifal*.

10. SOURCES

MANUSCRIPTS

The myth, originated by Wagner himself, that the text and music of his works were conceived in a simultaneous flight of inspiration has long since been demolished. It is true, of course, that text and music are fused indissolubly in Wagner's works – certainly in the mature music dramas – but the principle of fusion can be traced back to the point of conception only by a selective, and ideologically driven, reading of the evidence.

To separate the discussion of Wagner's textual and musical sources is therefore to do little violence to the artistic process. Wagner's general procedure in evolving a text for setting consisted of the following stages: an initial prose sketch (this stage applies only to the works from *Das Rheingold* onwards), an elaborated prose draft, a verse draft and a fair copy of the poem. Clearly it was the complexity of the mythological sources deployed in the *Ring* that persuaded Wagner of the need for a preliminary prose sketch for *Das Rheingold* and *Die Walküre*. The resulting documents outline the dramatic action in succinct manner and presage its final form with remarkable clear-sightedness. One or two less plausible initial inspirations – including that of Wotan revealed bathing in the Rhine in the opening scene of *Das Rheingold*, and witnessing the congress of Siegmund and Sieglinde in Act 1 of *Die Walküre* – were subsequently jettisoned. The latter notion was contained in a series of supplementary prose sketches that Wagner made for *Das Rheingold* and *Die Walküre* in a pocket notebook. For *Siegfried* (at that time called *Der junge Siegfried*), Wagner also made some brief, fragmentary prose sketches, but for *Götterdämmerung* (originally called *Siegfrieds Tod*) he made no prose sketch as such, having already organized the material for what was to become the whole cycle in a prose scenario of 1848, entitled *Der Nibelungen-Mythus: als Entwurf zu einem Drama*.

The first prose sketch of *Die Meistersinger*, dating from 1845, is a detailed scenario, with a coherent outline of the plot, lacking some key names (Walther, Eva and Beckmesser are called 'the young man', 'the girl' and 'the Marker') but frequently breaking into dialogue. The initial prose sketches for *Tristan* and *Parsifal* have not survived.

In his prose drafts (the first stage for *Der fliegende Holländer*, *Tannhäuser* and *Lohengrin*, the second for all subsequent operas) Wagner set down a detailed outline of the story, again punctuated by fragments of dialogue (still in prose form). Most important elements of the text are in place by this time, though Wagner was still capable of making radical changes at a later stage. There is, for example (Darcy, N 1993), no mention in the prose draft for *Das Rheingold* of either Wotan's emblematic spear or Loge's identity as the god of fire.

The next stage was the versification of the text, at which point any vestigial prose dialogue, and indeed the entire text, would be rendered in poetic verse: *Stabreim* (alliterative verse) in the case of the *Ring*, *Endreim* (end-rhyme) in the earlier operas, and a composite form in the later works. Examination of the relevant sources shows that sometimes Wagner would find the ideal wording immediately; on other occasions he would subject the text to considerable reworking. The scene directions were also expanded, sometimes revised, at this stage.

The final stage in the preparation of the text was that of the fair copy – an accurate description in Wagner's case, since his hand was elegant and his work generally free of corrections. Occasionally he did decide on late amendments and, if sufficiently radical, as in the case of *Siegfrieds Tod*, he would make a further fair copy; there were no fewer than four fair copies of the latter text.

The nomenclature of the musical sketches and drafts is a more problematic affair, partly because Wagner's compositional process altered over the course of his career, partly for ideological reasons (briefly, Wagner scholars of the protectionist school used to follow the composer in presenting *Der fliegende Holländer*, *Tannhäuser* and *Lohengrin* as incipient music dramas). Thus Otto Strobel, the Bayreuth archivist between the wars, used the terms *Kompositionsskizze* (composition sketch) and *Orchesterskizze* (orchestral sketch) indiscriminately for both the Romantic operas and the music dramas, implying moreover (erroneously) that the compositional process was limited to the first stage, while the second stage saw an immediate elaboration into an orchestral score. Strobel's terms held sway for several decades, though others were proposed in the 1960s and 70s. The nomenclature now generally established is that adopted by the *Wagner Werk-Verzeichnis*. For the early operas (*Die Feen*, *Das Liebesverbot* and *Rienzi*) and for *Der fliegende Holländer*, Wagner used various scraps of paper to jot down preliminary musical ideas, then sketching individual numbers or whole scenes. These sketches, sometimes in pencil, sometimes in ink, set the text generally using two staves – one for the vocal line, the other indicating the bass, occasionally with embryonic harmony in between. Then came the crucial complete draft, made in ink: a setting of an entire act, incorporating the preliminary sketches and filling in any gaps. For this draft Wagner added staves as required to show all the vocal and choral parts. The next, and final, stage for the four works in question was the making of a full score, a relatively easy process that could be undertaken whenever convenient, the real composition having already been completed.

For *Tannhäuser*, where Wagner began to move away from construction in numbers, he made a large number of sketches for individual sections – not necessarily in chronological order – next making a complete draft, which survives only in fragmentary form. In this case, a further complete draft preceded the making of the full score. For *Lohengrin*, apart from some preliminary sketching, Wagner went straight to a first complete draft, on two staves, working from the beginning to the end of an act, and following it with a second complete draft incorporating amendments and elaboration but stopping short of detailed orchestration. Here again Wagner moved direct to a full score.

His procedure in *Das Rheingold* was also to make a complete draft, in pencil, setting the text on one stave, with little more than a bass line on another stave (sometimes two). The need to elaborate the scoring of *Das Rheingold*, with its expanded orchestra, led Wagner to move next to a draft of a full score, initially (prelude) in ink and resembling a full score, but from Scene 1 in pencil and with staves added as necessary (the intermediate nature of this draft has led some scholars to term it 'instrumentation draft'). The final stage was a fair copy of the score.

Wagner began sustained work on *Die Walküre* with a complete draft that was elaborated to a greater degree than that for *Das Rheingold*, with the orchestral part sketched generally on two staves rather than one. He did not feel the need to make the same kind of draft full score as he had for *Das Rheingold*; however, because the composition of *Die Walküre* was extended over a much longer period, he had some difficulty remembering exactly what the 'unfamiliar hieroglyphics' of the complete draft stood for, with the result that some passages had to be recomposed.

Determined never to make the same mistake again, Wagner changed his procedure thereafter. Thus from *Siegfried* onwards he not only made two complete drafts, the second in ink, on at least three staves, before moving to a full score, but he also worked one act at a time, alternating between the two drafts.

With *Tristan* Wagner ensured that each act was completed and engraved before beginning the next. But for acts 2 and 3 of *Die Meistersinger*, as well as Act 3 of *Siegfried*, *Götterdämmerung* and *Parsifal*, he changed his procedure once again, in that the entire opera was finished in its second complete draft before the full score was begun. This second complete draft was, moreover, extremely elaborate – to the extent that it is sometimes called a 'short score'.

Most of Wagner's preliminary sketches and jottings – made on scraps of paper, in diaries or sometimes on manuscripts or copies of the poems – are undated and undatable. The complete drafts, on the other hand, are meticulously dated. With the exception of those in private collections, Wagner's surviving autograph manuscripts reside in libraries and archives in various locations in Europe and the USA. The majority are housed in the Nationalarchiv der Richard-Wagner-Stiftung in Bayreuth. Among the autographs that have not survived, the most celebrated are the scores of *Die Feen*, *Das Liebesverbot* and *Rienzi*, and the fair copies of *Das Rheingold* and *Die Walküre*. These were all presented to Ludwig II of Bavaria, from whose estate they passed to the Wittelsbacher Ausgleichsfond. The German Chamber of Industry and Commerce purchased them from the Ausgleichsfond and presented them to Hitler on his 50th birthday in 1939. It is assumed that they were destroyed in April 1945, though repeated rumours of their survival give cause to hope that they may one day resurface. In any case, 'the whole incident', in Darcy's words, 'must be judged as Hitler's final contribution to the cause of Wagner scholarship'.

PRINTED EDITIONS

The first 'complete edition' of Wagner's works was undertaken by Michael Balling and published by Breitkopf & Härtel between 1912 and 1929. Only ten of the projected 20 or more volumes appeared. A modern reprint was published by the Da Capo Press in 1971. The edition lacks several major scores, including those of *Rienzi*, *Der fliegende Holländer*, *Die Meistersinger*, *Parsifal* and all four *Ring* operas. On the other hand, it does include the early operas *Die Hochzeit* (only an introduction, chorus and septet were composed), *Die Feen* and *Das Liebesverbot*. (The editions of the first and last were the first to be printed.) Balling's edition of *Lohengrin* includes in a supplement the second part of the Grail Narration, which was cut by the composer before the première, and consequently omitted from the first printed, and all subsequent, editions. The Breitkopf project also includes valuable editions of the orchestral works, lieder, choral and piano music, as well as Wagner's interpolations for operas by Marschner, Blum and Bellini. Balling was hampered by the unavailability of many crucial sources and his edition, while creditable, falls short of modern critical standards.

The second complete edition, by contrast – still in progress – maintains the highest critical standards. *Richard Wagner: Sämtliche Werke* was initiated in 1970 by B. Schott's Söhne of Mainz, in cooperation with the Bavarian Academy of Fine Arts. The original general editors were Egon Voss and the late Carl Dahlhaus. Volumes i–xxi will contain the scores of all the works (including those uncompleted), volumes xxii–xxxi the relevant texts and documents associated with the stage works. The decision to opt for the original (1841) version – set in Scotland and with Senta's Ballad in A minor – in Isolde Vetter's scrupulous edition of *Der fliegende Holländer* is idiosyncratic, given that the work is very rarely performed in that version. Indeed, other volumes in the series have also been criticized – for example in terms of impracticable page turns – as being less useful for performing musicians than for scholars.

All the operas from *Der fliegende Holländer* to *Parsifal* are available both in the form of miniature scores (published by Eulenburg) and as full-size, softback reprints of selected early editions (published by Dover Publications Inc.). Editions of the *Ring* operas are bedevilled by the fact that not all of the alterations to the text made by Wagner subsequent to his 1853 limited edition – i.e. during the process of composition – found their way into the 1863 public printing and 1872 *Gesammelte Schriften* version of the libretto. As a result, the supposedly authoritative 1872 version – the *Gesammelte Schriften* were assembled under Wagner's own supervision – frequently corresponds neither to the earliest editions of the text nor to that found in the musical scores.

11. WAGNERISM

Even during Wagner's lifetime, appraisal of his achievement was clouded by political and ideological considerations, professional jealousies and extra-musical factors of various kinds. Thus was the pattern set for the next century and more, for rarely has a composer excited such extreme passions among cognoscenti and lay listeners alike.

The opera criticism of writers such as Fétis, Hanslick and J.W. Davison, publishing respectively in Paris, Vienna and London, can be dismissed as the reactionary, *parti pris* posturing for which the profession is celebrated, but it reflected an influential strand of public opinion which found Wagner's aesthetic theories hard to stomach. Davison himself came to a more measured view of Wagner when the *Ring* received its first staging in 1876, while his German-born colleague Francis Hueffer, who joined *The Times* in 1878, was an enthusiastic and well-informed proselytiser for the Wagnerian cause.

The fact that every cultural figure of any standing, from Marx to William Morris, and Ruskin to Tolstoy, had an opinion on Wagner and his music is indicative of the composer's influence, and if that particular quartet remained unconvinced of his genius, there were countless others who took a contrary view. The partisanship of Liszt, Wolf and Bruckner is well known, though Tchaikovsky, Grieg and Saint-Saëns were also among the first *Ring* audiences.

Nor was the polarity any less marked after Wagner's death. The intensity of Nietzsche's apostatic diatribes may be accounted for, in part, by neurosis and, finally, insanity, yet his arguments cannot be dismissed out of hand. Indeed, his exposition of a morally suspect, alluringly decadent art, that offered 'strange enchantments' and 'sweet infinities' even as it paralysed the intellect, is all the more poignant as that of a former acolyte who has lost his faith. Thomas Mann's later reflections on the subject were to echo Nietzsche's formulation, though Mann did not preclude the possibility of intellectual engagement as well as emotional.

Ironically, given Wagner's barely concealed antipathy to the country, France was from an early stage a significant outpost of Wagnerism. In the 1880s Wagner's music was a staple ingredient of the French orchestral repertory, thanks largely to the efforts of conductors such as Edouard Colonne and Charles Lamoureux, and in due course the operas came to be more frequently staged too. The doyen of 19th-century French music, César Franck, studied Wagner's scores closely and was clearly influenced by them, but he maintained a certain distance from the Wagner cult, deciding, for example, not to make the pilgrimage to Bayreuth. The master's disciples were less strong-willed, however. Guillaume Lekeu fainted during the Prelude to *Tristan* at the Bayreuth Festival and had to be carried out. Chabrier resigned his government post and became a composer on hearing *Tristan* in Munich; his opera *Gwendoline* is characterized by leitmotifs and other Wagnerian fingerprints. Chausson and Duparc are among other notable composers heavily influenced by Wagner.

Even less plausibly, Russia proved to be fertile Wagnerian territory too, in spite of the composer's tenuous association with the country in his lifetime. The spiritual dimension of his art struck a chord, however, with practitioners of the mystical, Symbolist-inspired movement that swept the country at the turn of the century. Wagner's theories and aesthetic ideas were actually discussed more than the works themselves were performed, and after the Revolution too it was the anti-capitalist tendency of such essays as *Die Kunst und die Revolution* that appealed to Bolsheviks and intellectuals alike. Mass festivals were organized, often involving thousands of people, in a grand synthesis of music, dance, rhythmic declamation and decorative arts that unmistakably, though tacitly – art of the past not being officially approved – invoked the spirit of the *Gesamtkunstwerk*.

In Britain, Wagner's music was much better known: the *Ring* was performed in London as early as 1882 and only with World War I did German music temporarily disappear from the repertory. The influence on the harmonic language of composers such as Parry, Stanford and Elgar is obvious, while in William Ashton Ellis, indefatigable translator and editor, Wagnerism found one of its most dedicated adherents. In America, too, there was passionate enthusiasm for Wagner's operas and a veritable cult developed with the expatriate conductor Anton Seidl at its centre.

Adulation of Wagner in Germany itself inevitably became entwined with the upsurge of Wilhelminian nationalism. Kaiser Wilhelm II visited and subsidized Bayreuth, and had his car horn tuned to a Wagnerian leitmotif. The spirit of 'Bayreuth Idealism' was enshrined in its most unadulterated form in the *Bayreuther Blätter*, the periodical established by Wagner and Hans von Wolzogen in 1878. Wolzogen's six-decade editorship ensured a platform for Germany's leading racists and anti-semites, who interpreted the canon, and especially *Parsifal*, as harbingers of a true Aryan culture. A regular contributor to the *Bayreuther Blätter* was Houston Stewart Chamberlain, whose *Grundlagen des 19. Jahrhunderts* was a formidably influential proto-Nazi tract. The association of Wagner's works with Hitler and the Third Reich was to cast a long shadow that had still not been completely dissipated by the end of the 20th century.

The impact of the music itself on composers of the late 19th and 20th centuries has been similarly wide-reaching. On one level, it can be detected in the rich harmonic language, unresolved dissonances, sequences and other technical features of late Romanticism, as exhibited by Elgar, Richard Strauss and Berg, to name but three. The use of leitmotifs and through-composed procedures in opera also became standard. On a more subtle level, it is possible also to trace Wagner's principles of 'musical prose' through Schoenberg to later modernists such as Boulez and Maxwell Davies, while other formal parallels can be seen in the work of Stockhausen and Berio. Ultimately, however, no composer of the post-Wagnerian period can be said to be untouched by his influence, even if only in a negative sense.

The impact of Wagner on the other arts, particularly literature and the visual arts, was no less crucial. Baudelaire was an early admirer of Wagner in France, and other Symbolists such as Verlaine and Mallarmé demonstrated their allegiance both in their poetry and in theoretical articles – the *Revue wagnérienne*, founded in 1885, provided an ideal forum. From the use of symbolism and leitmotif to stream of consciousness techniques it was but a short step, and if James Joyce and Virginia Woolf perfected the latter, then no one deployed leitmotif with more subtlety and ingenuity than Proust in *A la recherche du temps perdu*. Wagnerian symbolism and mythology permeate the novels of D.H. Lawrence and Thomas Mann, with a host of other writers, from Joseph Conrad to Anthony Burgess in the modern era, also paying their dues.

Countless minor artists of the 19th, and indeed 20th, centuries similarly paid allegiance to Wagner in canvases that echoed the themes, symbols and *mises-en-scène* of his operas. Among major artists, it was again the Parisian avant garde that set the pace. The terms 'Symbolist' and 'Wagnerian' were almost interchangeable when applied to such artists as Gustave Moreau and Odilon Redon, while Henri Fantin-Latour's lithographs and paintings of Wagnerian scenes dated back to the Impressionist era of the 1860s; Renoir too painted a pair of overdoor panels illustrating scenes from *Tannhäuser*. German and Austrian artists, such as Max Klinger and Gustav Klimt, received their inspiration from Wagner via the Parisians, while Aubrey Beardsley, Van Gogh, Gauguin and Cézanne all came under the Wagnerian spell. Kandinsky's experiments with synaesthesia were influenced in part by the work of Skryabin, but his desire to combine several arts in a *Bühnengesamtkunstwerk* unmistakably reflects the expansionist ambitions of Wagner.

WORKS

Editions: *Richard Wagner: Sämtliche Werke*, ed. C. Dahlhaus, E. Voss and others (Mainz, 1970–) [SW]
  Richard Wagners Werke, ed. M. Balling (Leipzig, 1912–29/R) [B; inc.]
Catalogue: J. Deathridge, M. Geck and E. Voss, eds.: *Wagner Werk-Verzeichnis (WWV): Verzeichnis der musikalischen Werke Richard Wagners und ihrer Quellen* (Mainz, 1986) [WWV]

Dates given for MS sources refer to the beginning and end of complete drafts only, including fair copies of librettos and full scores.

Dates in square brackets have been deduced from sources other than those mentioned in the same column. Full details of all autograph MSS (including single musical sketches prior to first complete drafts), copies in other hands as well as first and subsequent major prints are to be found in WWV. For a discussion of terminology see WWV (foreword) and J. Deathridge: 'The Nomenclature of Wagner's Sketches', *PRMA*, ci (1974–5), 75–83. All texts are by Wagner unless otherwise stated.

NA – *Nationalarchiv der Richard-Wagner-Stiftung, Bayreuth*   RWG – *Richard-Wagner-Gedenkstätte der Stadt Bayreuth*

Text MSS (autograph): ps – prose sketch (outline); pd – prose draft (detailed); vd – verse draft (subsequent prose or verse drafts are indicated by superscript numerals: pd^1, vd^2 etc.)

Music MSS (autograph): cd – complete draft (= single existing complete draft); fcd – first complete draft (outline); scd – second complete draft (detailed); fs – full score (= single existing full score); sfs – second full score (fair copy); pm – performance material; ffs – first full score (draft)

Prints: vs – vocal score; fs – full score; ps – piano score

Writings: *Gesammelte Schriften und Dichtungen*, i–x (Leipzig, 1871–83, 4/1907) [GS]
  Sämtliche Schriften und Dichtungen, i–xvi (Leipzig [1911–14]) [SS]
  Richard Wagner's Prose Works, ed. and trans. W.A. Ellis, i–viii (London, 1892–9/R) [PW]
  Das braune Buch: Tagebuchaufzeichnungen 1865–1882, ed. J. Bergfeld (Zürich and Freiburg, 1975; Eng. trans., London, 1980) [BB]

OPERAS, MUSIC DRAMAS

WWV	title	genre, acts, libretto	composition, sources	première	publication	dedication, remarks	
32	Die Feen	grosse romantische Oper, 3, after C. Gozzi: La donna serpente	text: pd, vd (both lost) [Jan–Feb 1833, Leipzig]; rev. dialogue, GB-Lbl, NA, vd¹, vd² [sum. 1834, Leipzig] music: cd, NA, fs (lost), Feb 1833–Jan 1834, Würzburg ov. (end): cd, 27 Dec 1833; fs, 6 Jan 1834 Act 1: 20 Feb–24 May 1833; fs (end), 6 Aug 1833 Act 2 (end): cd, 27 Sept 1833; fs, 1 Dec 1833 Act 3 (end): cd, 7 Dec 1833; fs, 1 Jan 1834	Munich, Kgl Hof- und National, 29 June 1888, cond. F. Fischer ov.: Magdeburg, 10 Jan 1835, cond. Wagner	lib.: Mannheim, 1888; SW xxii vs: Mannheim, 1888 fs: c1890 (orchestration rev. H. Levi); B xiii; SW i	pm (not autograph), D-Mbs, from lost fs or copy	2, 23, 24, 40, 41, 42
38	Das Liebesverbot, oder Die Novize von Palermo	grosse komische Oper, 2, after W. Shakespeare: Measure for Measure	text: pd (lost), vd, GB-Lbl [mid-June–Dec 1834, Rudolstadt and Magdeburg]; Fr. trans.: vd, Lbl [aut. 1839, Paris] music: cd, NA, fs (lost), Jan 1835–[March 1836], Magdeburg Act 1 (begin): cd, 23 Jan 1835 Act 2 (end): cd, 30 Dec 1835 arrs. from nos.2, 9, 11 (in Fr.): pm, NA [Feb–March 1840], Paris]	Magdeburg, Stadt, 29 March 1836, cond. Wagner; 2 duets from Act 1: Magdeburg, Stadt, 6 April 1835, cond. Wagner	lib. Leipzig, 1911/R1981; SW xxii vs: Leipzig, 1922/R1982 fs: B xiv; SW ii Karnevalslied, from no.11, vs (in Ger.): Stuttgart, 1837 Gesang der Isabella, from no.6, vs (in Ger.): Munich, 1896	copy of lost fs in Wittelsbacher Ausgleichsfonds, Munich	3, 4, 23, 24, 25, 37, 40, 41, 42

WWV	title	genre, acts, libretto	composition, sources	première	publication	dedication, remarks
49	Rienzi, der Letzte der Tribunen	grosse tragische Oper, 5, after E. Bulwer-Lytton: *Rienzi: the Last of the Roman Tribunes*	text: ps, *US-PHci*, pd, vd, NA [June/July 1837, Blasewitz and Dresden; June] –Aug 1838, Mitau and Riga; Fr. trans.: vd, NA [sum. 1839–wint. 1839–40] music: cd, NA, fs (lost), Aug 1838– Nov 1840, Riga and Paris ov.: 1st draft (begin), 20 Sept 1840; cd (end), 23 Oct 1840; fs (end) [19 Nov 1840] Act 1: cd, 7 Aug–6 Dec 1838; fs [8 Sept 1838]–6 Feb 1839 Act 2: cd, 6 Feb–9 April 1839; fs (end), 12 Sept 1839 Act 3: cd, 15 Feb–7 July 1840; fs, 6 June–11 Aug 1840 Act 4: cd, 10 July–29 Aug 1840; fs (begin), 14 Aug 1840 Act 5: cd, 5–19 Sept 1840 Prelude to Act 3 for perf. on 2 evenings [Jan 1843]: cd, private collection, fs, NA, *S-Smf*	Dresden, Kgl Sächsisches Hof, 20 Oct 1842, cond. K. Reissiger	lib: Dresden, 1842; Hamburg, 1844; Berlin, 1847; SW xxiii vs: Dresden, 1844 fs: Dresden, 1844 (shortened version); SW iii	Friedrich August II, King of Saxony; pm (inc., not autograph), *D-Dl*, from lost fs or copy; for Wagner's revs. see SW iii/5 and WWV 49 *Erläuterungen* 4, 5, 22, 23, 24, 25, 37, 40, 41, 42

WWV	title	genre, acts, libretto	composition, sources	première	publication	dedication, remarks
63	Der fliegende Holländer	romantische Oper, 3, after H. Heine: *Aus den Memoiren des Herren von Schnabelewopski*	text: pd (in Fr.), *F-Pn* [2–6 May 1840]; pd (in Ger.); RWG [early 1841]; vd (in Ger.), RWG, 18–28 May 1841, Meudon Senta's Ballad, Song of Scottish Sailors, Song of the Dutchman's Crew: vd (in Fr.), *GB-Lbl*, May–June 1840 music: cd (lost), fs, NA, July–Nov 1841, Meudon and Paris ov. (end): cd, 5 Nov 1841; fs [19 Nov 1841] Act 1 (begin): cd, 23 July 1841 Act 2 (end of Senta's Ballad): cd, 31 July 1841 Act 2 (begin no.5): cd, 4 Aug [1841] Act 2 (end): cd, 13 Aug [1841] Act 3 (end): cd, 22 Aug 1841; fs, 21 Oct 1841 Senta's Ballad, Song of Scottish Sailors, Song of the Dutchman's Crew: cd, fs (both partly lost), NA, RWG, *US-NYp* [May–July 1840] rev. end of ov., 1860: ffs, NA, 19 Jan 1860, sfs, *GB-Lbl* [shortly before 16 March 1860]	Dresden, Kgl Sächsisches Hof, 2 Jan 1843, cond. Wagner	lib: Dresden, 1843, Zürich, 1852; Munich, 1864; SW xxiv vs: Dresden, 1844; Berlin, 1909 (Weingartner version) fs: Dresden, 1844; Berlin, 1896 (Weingartner version); SW iv (orig. version with later alterations in separate vol.) ov. with rev. ending of 1860, fs: 1861	Ida von Lüttichau (née von Knobelsdorf); orig. version in 1 act; rev. 1846, 1852; ending modified 1860 4, 5, 9, 22, 23, 24, 25, 26, 27, 38, 39, 40, 42

WWV	title	genre, acts, libretto	composition, sources	première	publication	dedication, remarks	
70	Tannhäuser und der Sängerkrieg auf Wartburg	grosse romantische Oper, 3; 1859–60 version: Handlung, 3	text: stage 1: June 1842–April 1843, Aussig, Teplitz and Dresden; pd¹, NA (with orig. title 'Der Venusberg'), 28 June–6 July 1842; pd², NA, 8 July 1842 (end); vd¹ (lost); vd¹, NA [shortly before 7 April 1843 with later alterations] stage 2: [early 1847, Dresden]; pd, vd (lost) stage 3: [Sept 1859–Feb/March 1861, Paris]; vd¹, vd² (in Ger.), NA, private collection stage 4: [Aug/Sept 1861, Vienna–early 1865, Munich]; vd¹, vd² (both partly lost), Geheimarchiv, Munich music: stage 1: [July 1843]–April 1845, Teplitz and Dresden; preliminary sketches, private collections, D-LEu, Mbs, RWG, S-Smf; cd, private collection, NA; fs (destroyed during lithographing in 1845) ov. (end): cd, 11 Jan 1845 Act 1: cd, Nov 1843–27 Jan 1844 Act 2: cd, 7 Sept–15 Oct 1844 Act 3: cd, 19–29 Dec 1844, fs (end), 13 April 1845 stage 2: [Oct 1845]–May 1847, Dresden; cd, NA, 30 April 1847 (end); fs, NA, 7 May 1847 (end) stage 3: [Aug/Sept 1860–March 1861, Paris] Act 1 scene i: cd, NA, fs, NA, 28 Jan 1861 (end); Act 1 scene ii: fcd, NA, scd, NA, 18 Oct 1860 (end), fs, NA: further MSS in A-Wn, D-Mbs, NA, RWG, Wagnermuseum, Eisenach, F-Pn, Po stage 4: [probably aut. 1861, Vienna–sum. 1867, Munich]; fs (partly autograph), private collection, pm (not autograph), D-Mbs	stage 1: Dresden, Kgl Sächsisches Hof, 19 Oct 1845, cond. Wagner stage 2: Dresden, Kgl Sächsisches Hof, 1 Aug 1847, cond. Wagner stage 3: Paris, Opéra, 13 March 1861, cond. L. Dietsch stage 4: Munich, Kgl Hof- und National, 1 Aug 1867, cond. H. von Bülow	stage 1 lib: Dresden, 1845; SW xxv vs: Dresden, 1846; SW xx/1 fs: Dresden, 1845; B iii; SW v stage 2 lib: Dresden, 1847; SW xxv vs: Dresden, 1852 fs: Dresden, 1860, B iii; SW v stage 3 lib: Paris, 1861; SW xxv vs: Paris, 1861 fs: B iii; SW vi stage 4 lib: Munich, 1867; SW xxv vs: Berlin and Dresden, 1876 fs: Berlin, c1888; B iii; SW vi	Camille Erard (stage 2, 1860); see WWV 70 *Erläuterungen*	5, 9, 11, 23, 26, 27, 33, 39, 40

WWV	title	genre, acts, libretto	composition, sources	première	publication	dedication, remarks
75	Lohengrin	romantische Oper, 3	text: pd, NA, 3 Aug 1845, Marienbad (end); vd, private collection, 27 Nov 1845 [Dresden] (end) music: fcd (partly lost), private collections, *D-Mbs*, NA, *US-NYp*, *STu*; scd, NA; fs, NA; [May 1846]–April 1848, Dresden Prelude: scd (end), 29 Aug [1847], fs, (begin), 1 Jan 1848 Act 1: scd, 12 May–8 June 1847 Act 2: scd, 18 June–2 Aug 1847 Act 3: fcd (end), 30 July 1846; scd, 9 Sept 1846–5 March 1847; fs (end), 28 April 1848 arrs. for concerts in Zürich, May 1853, (mostly lost), NA arrs. for concerts in St Petersburg and Budapest, 1863, NA, *H-Bo*, private collection	Weimar, Grossherzogliches Hof, 28 Aug 1850, cond. Liszt Act 1 finale (in concert): Dresden, Kgl Sächsisches Hof, 22 Sept 1848, cond. Wagner	lib: Weimar, 1850; SW xxvi vs: Leipzig, 1851 fs: Leipzig, 1852; B iv; SW vii	Liszt; Prelude comp. last but orchd first; orig. version of lib. in SW xxvi	6, 9, 23, 26, 27, 28, 32, 37, 39, 40, 42
86	Der Ring des Nibelungen	Bühnenfestspiel für drei Tage und einen Vorabend		as a cycle: Bayreuth, Festspielhaus, 13, 14, 16, 17 Aug 1876, cond. H. Richter		'Im vertrauen auf den deutschen Geist entworfen und zum Ruhme seines erhabenen Wohlthäters des Königs Ludwig II von Bayern vollender'	6, 7, 10, 23, 27, 28, 29, 36, 37, 38, 39, 42, 43, 44
86a	Das Rheingold	Vorabend	text: ps, pd, vd, NA [Oct/Nov 1851]–Nov 1852, Albisbrunn and Zürich; pd, 23–31 March 1852; vd, 15 Sept–3 Nov 1852 music: cd, NA, ffs (partly lost), NA, *US-NYp*, *PRæ*; sfs (lost) Nov 1853–Sept 1854, Zürich; cd, 1 Nov 1853–14 Jan 1854; ffs, 1 Feb–28 May 1854; sfs, 15 Feb–26 Sept 1854 arrs. for concerts in Vienna, 1862–3, private collection, *A-Wgm*	Munich, Kgl Hof- und National, 22 Sept 1869, cond. F. Wüllner excerpts from scenes i, ii, iv (in concert): Vienna, An der Wien, 26 Dec 1862, cond. Wagner	lib.: Zürich, 1853; SW xxix/2 vs: Mainz, 1861 fs: Mainz, 1873; SW x	copy by Friedrich Wölfel of lost fs, NA; pm for 1st perf. (*not* autograph), *D-Mbs*	10, 13, 20, 24, 27, 28, 39, 40, 41

WWV	title	genre, acts, libretto	composition, sources	première	publication	dedication, remarks	
86b	Die Walküre	erster Tag, 3	text: ps, pd, vd, NA [Nov/Dec 1851]–July 1852, Albisbrunn and Zürich Act 1: pd (begin), 17 May 1852; vd, 1–11 June [1852] Act 2: vd, 12–23 June [1852] Act 3: (end): pd, 26 May 1852; vd, 1 July 1852 music: cd, ffs, NA, sfs (lost), June 1854–March 1856, Zürich, London, Seelisberg and Zürich Act 1: cd, 28 June–1 Sept 1854; ffs (end), 3 April 1855; sfs (begin), 14 July 1855 Act 2: cd, 4 Sept–18 Nov 1854; ffs, 7 April–20 Sept 1855 Act 3: cd, 20 Nov–27 Dec 1854; ffs, 8 Oct 1855–20 March 1856; sfs (end), 23 March 1856 arrs. for concerts in Vienna, 1862–3, private collection, *A-Wgm*, NA, RWG, *US-NYpm*, *Wc*	Munich, Kgl Hof- und National, 26 June 1870, cond. Wüllner excerpts from Acts 1, 3 (in concert): Vienna, An der Wien, 26 Dec 1862, cond. Wagner	lib: Zürich, 1853; SW xxix/2 vs: Mainz, 1865 fs: Mainz, 1874; SW xi 'Walkürenritt': Mainz, 1876	copy by Alois Niest of lost sfs, *D-Mbs*; 'Walkürenritt', 'Winterstürme wichen dem Wonnemond', arr. pf by C. Tausig (1863, 1866) approved by Wagner but not identical with his arrs.	10, 13, 27, 28, 38, 39. 41

WWV	title	genre, acts, libretto	composition, sources	première	publication	dedication, remarks
86c	Siegfried	zweiter Tag, 3	text: ps, pd, NA, vd¹, private collection, vd²; NA, May 1851–[Nov/Dec 1852]; pd, 24 May–1 June 1851; vd¹, 3–24 June 1851 [1st rev, Nov/Dec 1852, 2nd rev, 1856] music: fcd, scd, ffs, sfs (Acts 1–2 only), NA [Sept 1856]–Aug 1857, Zürich (end scd Act 2); Dec 1864–Dec 1865, Munich (ffs Act 2); March 1869–Feb 1871, Tribschen (Act 3) Act 1: fcd (end), 20 Jan 1857; scd, 22 Sept 1856–5 Feb 1857; ffs, 11 Oct 1856–31 March 1857; sfs (begin), 12 May 1857 Act 2: fcd, 22 May–30 July 1857; scd, 18 June–9 Aug 1857; ffs, 22 Dec 1864–2 Dec 1865; sfs (end), 23 Feb 1869 Act 3: fcd, 1 March–14 June 1869; scd, 25 June–5 Aug 1869; ffs, 25 Aug 1869–5 Feb 1871 arrs. of 'Schmiedelieder' for concert in Vienna, 1863, NA, RWG, H-Bo	Bayreuth, Festspielhaus, 16 Aug 1876, cond. Richter 2 'Schmiedelieder' from Act 1 (in concert): Vienna, An der Wien, 1 Jan 1863, cond. Wagner	lib: Zürich, 1853; SW xxix/2 vs: Mainz, 1871 fs: Mainz, 1875; SW xii	11, 27, 28, 37, 39, 40, 41

Richard Wagner in Paris:
drawing by Ernst Benedikt Kietz,
pencil, 1840–42

Beginning of Act 3 of Wagner's 'Tristan und Isolde' in the developed draft
(orchestral sketch), page dated 1 May 1859
(Richard-Wagner-Museum, Bayreuth)

Richard Wagner at Tribschen, 1867

Richard, Cosima and Siegfried Wagner
at Bayreuth, c1873

Scene from Act 1 of Wagner's 'Tristan und Isolde', Hof- und Nationaltheater, Munich,
1865: lithograph by Michael Echter after stage design by Angelo Quaglio, 1867

Wagner receives the homage of Ernst von Weber and the animal kingdom (including Fafner the dragon) after the publication of his open letter against vivisection: caricature by C. von Grimm, 1879

'The effects of Wagner on the listener', Munich: lithograph by Honoré Daumier

Part of Senta's ballad from the autograph full score of Wagner's
'Der fliegende Holländer', composed 1841 (Richard-Wagner-Museum, Bayreuth)

'Die Meistersinger': beginning of Act 1 scene i in the developed draft
(orchestral sketch), 1862 (Richard-Wagner-Museum, Bayreuth)

Part of the first page (with sketch for the Sailor's song) from the prose sketch of Wagner's 'Tristan und Isolde', 1857 (Richard-Wagner-Museum, Bayreuth)

Beginning of the preliminary draft (composition sketch) for the opening scene with
Alberich and the Rhinemaidens in Wagner's 'Das Rheingold',
page dated 1 November 1853 (Richard-Wagner-Museum, Bayreuth)

WWV	title	genre, acts, libretto	composition, sources	première	publication	dedication, remarks	
86d	Götterdämmerung	dritter Tag, Vorspiel, 3	text: pd, NA, vd¹, private collection, vd², CH-W, vd³, NA, Oct 1848–Dec 1852, Dresden and Zürich; pd (end), Oct 1848 [prol. late Oct 1848]; vd¹, 12–28 Nov 1848; vd² [late 1848/early 1849]; vd³ (end), 15 Dec 1852 [1st rev., 1848/9; 2nd rev., Nov/Dec 1852] music: fcd, scd, fs, NA, Oct 1869–Nov 1874, Tribschen and Bayreuth Prol. (begin): fcd, 2 Oct 1869; scd, 11 Jan 1870; fs, 3 May 1873 Act 1: fcd, 7 Feb–5 June 1870; scd (end), 2 July 1870; fs (end), 24 Dec 1873 Act 2: fcd, 24 June–25 Oct 1871; scd, 5 July–19 Nov 1871; fs (end), 26 June 1874 Act 3: fcd, 4 Jan–10 April 1872; scd, 9 Feb–22 July 1872; fs, 10 June–21 Nov 1874	Bayreuth, Festspielhaus, 17 Aug 1876, cond. Richter excerpts from prol., Acts 1, 3 (in concert): Vienna, Musikvereinssaal, 25 March 1875, cond. Wagner	lib: Zürich, 1853; SW xxix/2 vs: Mainz, 1875 fs: Mainz, 1876; SW xiii	musical sketches and 2 inc. drafts of prol. (1 dated 12 Aug 1850), 1850, US-Wc, private collection	7, 14, 27, 28, 29, 38, 39, 41
90	Tristan und Isolde	Handlung, 3	text: ps, pd, vd, NA [aut. 1854]–Sept 1857, Zürich; pd (begin), 20 Aug 1857; vd (end), 18 Sept 1857 music: fcd, scd, fs, NA, Oct 1857–Aug 1859, Zürich, Venice and Lucerne Act 1 (with Prelude): fcd, 1 Oct–31 Dec 1857; scd, 5 Nov 1857–13 Jan 1858 Act 2: fcd, 4 May–1 July 1858; scd, 5 July 1858–9 March 1859; fs (end), 18 March 1859 Act 3: fcd, 9 April–16 July 1859; scd, 1 May–19 July 1859; fs (end), 6 Aug 1859 concert ending to Prelude: Dec 1859, Paris	Munich, Kgl Hof- und National, 10 June 1865, cond. Bülow Prelude (with concert ending): Prague, 12 March 1859, cond. Bülow Prelude (with concert ending): Paris, Italien, 25 Jan 1860, cond. Wagner	lib: Leipzig, 1859; SW xxvii vs: Leipzig, 1860 fs: Leipzig, 1860; B v; SW viii Prelude with Wagner's concert ending: Leipzig, 1860	earliest dated sketches 19 Dec 1856; practice of ending Prelude with conclusion of Act 3 introduced by Wagner, St Petersburg, 26 Feb 1863	11, 12, 29, 30, 35, 38, 39, 41, 43, 44

WWV	title	genre, acts, libretto	composition, sources	première	publication	dedication, remarks
96	Die Meistersinger von Nürnberg	3	text: pd¹ (end), 16 July 1845, Marienbad; pd², pd³, vd, NA, Schott, Mainz, Nov 1861–Jan 1862, Vienna and Paris Act 1 (end): vd, 5 Jan 1862 Act 2 (end): vd, 16 Jan 1862 Act 3 (end): pd³, 18 Nov 1861; vd, 25 Jan 1862 music: fcd, scd, NA, fs, *D-Ngm*, April–Dec 1862, Biebrich and Vienna; Feb 1866–Oct 1867, Geneva and Tribschen Prelude: scd, 13–20 April 1862; fs (begin) [3 June 1862] Act 1 (end): fcd [Feb 1866]; scd, 21 Feb 1866; fs, 23 March 1866 Act 2: fcd, 15 May–6 Sept 1866; scd, 8 June–23 Sept 1866; fs, 22 March–22 June 1867 Act 3: fcd, 2 Oct 1866–7 Feb 1867; scd, 8 Oct 1866–5 March 1867; fs, 26 June–24 Oct 1867 concert ending to Walther's Trial Song from Act 1: 12 July 1865, Munich	Munich, Kgl Hof- und National, 21 June 1868, cond. Bülow Prelude: Leipzig, Gewandhaus, 1 Nov 1862, cond. Wagner 'Versammlung der Meistersingerzunft' and Walther's Trial Song from Act 1: Vienna, An der Wien, 26 Dec 1862, cond. Wagner conclusion of Act 3 (from Hans Sachs's 'Verachtet mir die Meister nicht'): Linz, 4 April 1868, cond. Bruckner	lib: Mainz, 1862, SW xxviii vs: Mainz, 1868 fs: Mainz, 1868; SW ix Prelude, fs: Mainz, 1866	King Ludwig II of Bavaria; earliest dated sketch ('Wach auf' chorus) Jan 1862; entitled 'Komische Oper' in pd¹, 'Grosse Komische Oper' in pd² and pd³, 'Oper' in poster for 1st perf.

6, 11, 13, 23, 27, 29, 30, 38, 39, 41, 42

WWV	title	genre, acts, libretto	composition, sources	première	publication	dedication, remarks
111	Parsifal	Bühnenweihfestspiel, 3	text: ps (lost), pd¹, RWG, pd², vd, NA, April 1857, Zürich; Aug 1865, Munich; [Jan]–April 1877, Bayreuth; ps, end of April (not Good Friday, see SW xxx); pd¹, 27–30 Aug [1865]; pd² (end), 23 Feb 1877; vd (end), 19 April 1877 music: fcd, scd, fs, NA [Sept 1877]–Dec 1881, Bayreuth and Palermo Act 1: fcd (end), 29 Jan 1878; scd, 25 Sept 1877–31 Jan 1878; fs, 23 Aug 1879–25 April 1881 Act 2: fcd (end), 30 Sept [1878]; scd, 13 March–11 Oct 1878; fs, 6 June–20 Oct 1881 Act 3: fcd, 30 Oct 1878–16 April [1879]; scd, 14 Nov 1878–26 April 1879; fs, 8 Nov–25 Dec 1881	Bayreuth, Festspielhaus, 26 July 1882, cond. Levi Prelude: Bayreuth, 25 Dec 1878, cond. Wagner	lib: Mainz, 1877; SW xxx vs: Mainz, 1882 fs: Mainz, 1883; SW xiv	10, 15, 16, 20, 21, 24, 30, 31, 36, 37, 38, 39, 41, 42, 44

INCOMPLETE OR PROJECTED STAGE WORKS

WWV

1	Leubald (Trauerspiel, 5), 1826–8 (extracts from Act 5: Leipzig, 1908); SS xvi (extracts), SW xxxi (complete); no music survives (?none written)	1, 35
6	Pastoral opera (Schäferoper), after J.W. von Goethe: *Die Laune des Verliebten*, ? early 1830, lost	2
31	Die Hochzeit (Oper, ?3, after J. Büsching: *Ritterzeit und Ritterwesen*), Oct/Nov 1832–1 March 1833; B xii, SW xv; poem lost; of music, only introduction, chorus and septet written	2, 36, 42
40	Die hohe Braut (grosse Oper, 4 [5 in ps], after H. Koenig: *Die hohe Braut*), ?July 1836, Aug 1842 (Prague, 1848); SS xi, SW xxxi; music not set; no sketches survive. Wagner offered lib to K. Reissiger, then Hiller; finally set by J.B. Kittl as Bianca und Giuseppe, oder Die Franzosen vor Nizza	3, 36
48	Männerlist grösser als Frauenlist, oder Die glückliche Bärenfamilie (komische Oper, 2, after *The Thousand and One Nights*), ?sum. 1838; SS xi, SW xxxi; intended as Singspiel, with prose dialogue and individual numbers; hitherto unknown prose draft and sketches of 3 numbers (Introduction, Duet and Trio) resurfaced in 1994	3, 36
66	Die Sarazenin (Oper, 5), probably 1841, early 1843 (pd [now lost]: Bayreuth, 1889); SS xi, PW viii, SW xxxi (pd)	36
67	Die Bergwerke zu Falun (Oper, 3, after story by E.T.A. Hoffmann), Feb–Mar 1842 (scenario only: Bayreuth, 1905); SS xi, SW xxxi; scenario written for J. Dessauer; later offered to A. Röckel, who appears to have intended to set it. Wagner himself made no setting	36
76	Friedrich I. ([?opera], 5), Oct 1846, wint. 1848–9; SS xi, SW xxxi; scenario frag.; planned as opera, but not set, and no sketches survive	7, 23, 36
80	Jesus von Nazareth ([?opera], 5), Jan–April 1849 (pd: Leipzig, 1887); SS xi, PW viii, SW xxxi; 5-act scenario completed; not set, but 1 musical sketch survives	7, 23, 36
81	Achilleus ([?opera], 3), early 1849, Feb–July 1850; notes on *Achilleus* (Leipzig, 1885, SS xii, PW viii) may relate to projected theoretical essay rather than opera	7, 36
82	Wieland der Schmied (Heldenoper, 3), Dec 1849–March 1850 (pds: GS iii, SS iii, PW i, SW xxxi). Scenario only; offered to Berlioz (via Liszt), A. Röckel and W. Weissheimer, but none set it. Wagner himself made no setting; no musical sketches survive	7, 23, 36
89	Die Sieger ([opera], 3), May 1856 (ps: Leipzig, 1885, SS xi, PW viii, SW xxxi). Wagner still planning composition in 1878	10, 36
99	Luthers Hochzeit [?drama], August 1868 (ps: Bayreuth, 1937, SW xxxi); only prose sketches exist. Wagner appears not to have attempted to compose music; in 1878 considered prose play on subject	21, 36
100	[Lustspiel], 1, Aug 1868 (ps: Zürich and Freiburg, 1975, SW xxxi); only prose scenario exists, but some musical treatment may have been intended	
102	Eine Kapitulation (Lustspiel in antiker Manier), Nov 1870 (text: GS ix, SS ix, PW v, SW xxxi); text not set by Wagner, but he may have retouched setting by Richter, which has not survived (possibly destroyed by Richter)	13, 21, 36

ORCHESTRAL

10	Overture (Paukenschlag-Ouvertüre), B♭, sum. 1830, Leipzig, 25 Dec 1830, lost	
11	Overture (Politische Ouvertüre), ?Sept 1830, lost and ?inc.	
12	Overture to Die Braut von Messina (F. von Schiller), sum, or aut. 1830, ?lost	
13	Orch work, e, frag., ?1830 (possibly to be identified with WWV 12); SW xviii/1	
14	Overture, C (in 6/8 time), end 1830, lost	33
17	Overture, E♭, early 1831, lost and ?inc.	
20	Overture (Concert Overture no.1), d, sum./aut. 1831, Leipzig, 25 Dec 1831; B xx, SW xviii/1	
24	Overture, e, and incidental music to König Enzio (E. Raupach), wint. 1831–2, Leipzig, 17 Feb 1832 (Leipzig, 1907), SW xviii/1	
25	Entreactes tragiques, no.1, D, no.2, c, probably early 1832, SW xviii/1	
27	Concert Overture no.2, C♯ March 1832, Leipzig, ?end March 1832; B xx, SW xviii/1	
29	Symphony, C, ?April–June 1832, Prague, Nov 1832 (Leipzig, 1911), B xx, SW xviii/1	2, 31
35	Symphony, E, inc. [1st movt and 29 bars of Adagio], sketches orch. F. Mottl, Aug–Sept 1834, Munich, 13 Oct 1988	31
37	Overture, E♭, and incidental music to Columbus (T. Apel), Dec 1834–Jan 1835, Magdeburg, 16 Feb 1835 (Leipzig, 1907); SW xviii/2	31, 37
39	Overture, 'Polonia', C, May–July 1836, Königsberg, ?wint. 1836–7 (Leipzig, 1907); SW xviii/2	
41	Incidental music to Die letzte Heidenverschwörung in Preussen (J. Singer), frag., ?Feb 1837, Königsberg, ?17 Feb 1837; SW xv	
42	Overture 'Rule Britannia', D, March 1837, Riga, ?19 March 1838 (Leipzig, 1907); SW xviii/2	31, 37
59	Eine Faust-Ouvertüre (J.W. von Goethe), d, Dec 1839–Jan 1840, rev. Jan 1855, Dresden, 22 July 1844 (1st version), Zürich, 23 Jan 1855 (2nd version) (Leipzig, 1855); B xviii, SW xviii/2/3	24, 31
73	Trauermusik, on motifs from C.M. von Weber's Euryanthe, Nov 1844, Dresden, 14 Dec 1844; B xx, SW xviii/2	33
78	Symphonies (sketches only), 1846–7	32
97	Huldigungsmarsch, E♭, Aug 1864, Munich, 5 Oct 1864 (version for military band) (Mainz, 1890); Vienna, 12 Nov 1871 (orch version) (Mainz, 1871); B xviii, SW xviii/3	32
98	Romeo und Julie (sketches only), spr. 1868 (Karlsruhe, 1943); SW xxi	21
103	Siegfried Idyll, E, end Nov–Dec 1870, Tribschen, 25 Dec 1870 (Mainz, 1878); B, xviii, SW xviii/3	21, 32

WWV

104   Kaisermarsch, B♭, with unison 'people's chorus' ad lib, Feb–mid-March 1871, Berlin, 14 April 1871   32
(Leipzig, 1871); B xviii, SW xviii/3

107   Plans for overtures and symphonies (inc.); themes and melodies, 1874–83, incl. sketch in E♭ inscribed by
Cosima Wagner as 'Melodie der Porazzi', 1882, and theme in C marked 'Tempo di Porazzi', 1882

110   Grosser Festmarsch (Centennial March), G, Feb–March 1876, Philadelphia, 10 May 1876 (Mainz, 1876); B   32
xviii, SW xviii/3

CHAMBER

4   String Quartet, D, aut. 1829, lost   34
—   'Starnberg' Quartet. No evidence survives of such a work. See Millington, 1992   34
—   Adagio for clarinet and string quintet, formerly attrib. Wagner; in fact by H.J. Baermann, belonging to   34
Clarinet Quintet op.23; B xx

CHORAL

19   Two fugues, 4-pt unacc. chorus, aut. 1831–wint. 1831/2. No.1 set to words 'Dein ist das Reich'; no.2 has no
text; SW xvi/xxi

36   Incidental music to Beim Antritt des neuen Jahres 1835 (W. Schmale), SATB, orch, Dec 1834, Magdeburg,   33
1 Jan 1835; B xvi, SW xvi; music reset to new text by P. Cornelius for Wagner's 60th birthday, 1873

44   Nicolay ('Volks-Hymne'), S/T, SATB, orch, aut. 1837, Riga, 21 Nov 1837; B xvi, SW xvi   33

51   Gesang am Grabe, ?male chorus, Dec 1838–Jan 1839, Riga, 4 Jan 1839, lost

65   Descendons gaiment la courtille (chorus for M. Dumersan and C.-D. Dupeuty: La descente de la courtille),   33
SSTB, orch, ?Jan 1841, ?Paris, 20 Jan 1841

68   Der Tag erscheint, TTBB, May 1843, Dresden, 7 June 1843 (Berlin, 1906), rev. for male chorus and brass   5, 33
insts, ?May 1843; B xvi, SW xvi

69   Das Liebesmahl der Apostel ('eine biblische Szene'), male vv, orch, April–June 1843, Dresden, 6 July 1843   5, 33
(Leipzig, 1845); B xvi, SW xvi

71   Gruss seiner Treuen an Friedrich August den Geliebten, TTBB, wind band, Aug 1844, Pillnitz, 12 Aug   5, 33
1844 (Dresden, 1844: unacc. version); B xvi, SW xvi. Version for 1v, pf, Aug 1844; B xv, SW xvii

72   An Webers Grabe ('Hebt an den Sang'), TTBB, Nov 1844, Dresden, 15 Dec 1844 (Leipzig, 1872); B xvi,   5, 33
SW xvi

101   Wahlspruch für die deutsche Feuerwehr, TTBB, Nov 1869 (Speyer, 1870); SW xvi   34

106   Kinder-Katechismus, children's vv (soloists and unison chorus), pf, Dec 1873, Bayreuth, 25 Dec 1873; SW   34
xxi. Rev. version with orch acc., Dec 1874, Bayreuth, 25 Dec 1874 (Mainz, 1937); SW xxi

112   Willkommen in Wahnfried, du heil'ger Christ, children's vv, Dec 1877, Bayreuth, 24 Dec 1877; SW xxi   34

113   Ihr Kinder, geschwinde, geschwinde ('antiker Chorgesang'), children's vv, ?Dec 1880, Bayreuth, 25 Dec   34
1880; SW xxi

SONGS AND ARIAS

7   Songs, 1v, pf, 1828–30, frag. sketches and drafts only, possibly intended for the 'pastoral opera' (WWV 6)
or for theatrical perfs. involving Wagner's sisters, notably Rosalie; SW xxi

3   Aria, ?1v, pf, 1829, lost; arr. wind band and played in Kintschy's Swiss Chalet (Mein Leben)

8   Aria, S, orch, ? early 1830, lost; ?intended for 'pastoral opera' (WWV 6); ?identical with WWV 3

15   7 pieces for Goethe's Faust: 1 Lied der Soldaten, male vv, pf; 2 Bauer unter der Linde, S, T, mixed vv, pf; 3   34
Branders Lied, B, unison male vv, pf; 4 Lied des Mephistopheles ('Es war einmal ein König'), B, unison male
vv, pf; 5 Lied des Mephistopheles ('Was machst du mir vor Liebchens Tür'), B, pf; 6 Gretchen am Spinnrade,
S, pf; 7 Melodram, speaking role (Gretchen), pf; early 1831, B xv, SW xvii; ?written for perf. of play, Leipzig

28   Scene and Aria, S, orch, early 1832, Leipzig, 22 April 1832, lost; Abraham's thesis (1969) that aria was first
version of Ada's 'Ich sollte ihm entsagen' in Die Feen has been discounted (Deathridge, N 1978)

30   Glockentöne (Abendglocken) (T. Apel), 1v, pf, Oct 1832, lost

33   'Doch jetzt wohin ich blicke' (new allegro section for aria in Marschner: Der Vampyr), T, orch, Sept 1833,   34
Würzburg, 29 Sept 1833; B xv, SW xv

43   'Sanfte Wehmut will sich regen' (K. von Holtei, aria for C. Blum: Mary, Max und Michel), B, orch, Aug   34
1837, Riga, 1 Sept 1837; B xv, SW xv

45   Aria for J. Weigl: Die Schweizerfamilie, B, orch, ?Dec 1837, Riga, ?22 Dec 1837; composition draft resur-   34
faced in 1994

50   Der Tannenbaum (G. Scheurlin), ?aut. 1838 (Stuttgart, 1839), B xv, SW xvii

52   'Norma il predisse, O Druidi' (aria for V. Bellini: Norma), B, male vv (TB), orch, Sept/Oct 1839; B xv, SW   34
xv

53   Dors mon enfant, 1v, pf, aut. 1839 (Stuttgart, 1841); B xv, SW xvii   35

54   Extase (V. Hugo), 1v, pf, aut. 1839, frag.; SW xvii   35

55   Attente (Hugo), 1v, pf, aut. 1839 (Stuttgart, 1842); B xv, SW xvii   35

56   La tombe dit à la rose (Hugo), 1v, pf, aut. 1839, frag.; SW xvii   35

57   Mignonne (P. de Ronsard), 1v, pf, aut. 1839 (Stuttgart, 1843); B xv, SW xvii   35

58   Tout n'est qu'images fugitives (Soupir) (J. Reboul), 1v, pf, aut. 1839; B xv, SW xvii   35

60   Les deux grenadiers (H. Heine, trans., F.-A. Loeve-Veimars), Bar, pf, Dec 1839–early 1840 (Paris, 1840); B   35
xv, SW xvii

WWV

61	Adieux de Marie Stuart (P.-J. de Béranger), S, pf, March 1840 (Paris, 1913); B xv, SW xvii	35
91	Fünf Gedichte für eine Frauenstimme (Wesendonck Lieder) (M. Wesendonck), S, pf: 1 Der Engel, 2 Stehe still!, 3 Im Treibhaus, 4 Schmerzen, 5 Träume [order of 1st publication and usual perf.], Nov. 1857–May 1858 (1st version), Dec 1857–Oct 1858 (2nd version), Oct 1858 (3rd version), Laubenheim, nr Mainz, 30 July 1862 (Mainz, 1862); B xv, SW xvii. Träume arr. Wagner, solo vn, chamber orch (WWV 91b), Dec 1857, Zürich, 23 Dec 1857 (Mainz, 1878); B xx, SW xviii/3. Remainder arr. S, orch by F. Mottl and H.W. Henze (1976). Im Treibhaus and Träume both designated 'Studie zu Tristan und Isolde' by Wagner	35
92	Es ist bestimmt in Gottes Rat (Baron E. von Feuchtersleben), 1v, pf, probably Jan 1858, draft (13 bars)	
—	Schlaf, Kindchen, schlafe, Dec 1868 (Zürich and Freiburg, 1975). Lullaby headed 'Sylvester 68–69', using theme to reappear in Siegfried Idyll, incorporated in Annals	
105	Der Worte viele sind gemacht, 1v, April 1871 (Leipzig, 1871); SW xxi; title 'Kraft-Lied' inauthentic	

PIANO

for 2 hands unless otherwise stated

2	Sonata, d, sum. 1829, lost	
5	Sonata, f, aut. 1829, lost	
16	Sonata, B♭, 4 hands, early 1831, later orchd, lost	
21	Sonata, B♭, op.1, aut. 1831 (Leipzig, 1832); SW xix	35
22	Fantasia, f♯, aut. 1831 (Leipzig, 1905); SW xix	35
23a	Polonaise, D, end 1831–early 1832 (London, 1973); SW xxi	
23b	Polonaise, D, op.2, rev. of WWV 23a for 4 hands (Leipzig, 1832); SW xix	35
26	Grosse Sonate, A, op.4, early 1832 (Cologne, 1960); SW xix	
64	Albumblatt, E ('Albumblatt für E.B. Kietz "Lied ohne Worte"'), ?Dec 1840 (Vienna, 1911); SW xix	35
84	Polka, G, May 1853; SW xix	
85	Eine Sonate für das Album von Frau M[athilde] W[esendonck], A♭, June 1853 (Mainz, 1878); SW xix	35
88	Züricher Vielliebchen-Walzer, E♭, May 1854 (Berlin, 1901–2); SW xix	
93	Theme, A♭ [incorrectly known as 'Porazzi Theme'], ?1858, rev. 1881, SW xxi. For true 'Porazzi Theme' see ORCHESTRAL, WWV 107	
94	In das Album der Fürstin M[etternich], C, June 1861 (Leipzig, 1871); SW xix	35
95	Ankunft bei den schwarzen Schwänen, A♭, July 1861 (Leipzig, 1897); SW xix	35
108	Albumblatt, E♭, Jan–1 Feb 1875 (Mainz, 1876); SW xix	35

EDITIONS AND ARRANGEMENTS

9	L. van Beethoven: Sym. no.9, pf, sum. 1830–Easter 1831; SW xx/i	2
18	J. Haydn: Sym. no.103, pf, sum. 1831, lost	
34	V. Bellini: cavatina from Il pirata, orch, Nov–Dec 1833, lost	
46a	V. Bellini: Norma, retouching of orch, ?Dec 1837, Riga, ?11 Dec 1837; SW xx/iii	
47	G. Rossini: 'Li marinari' from Les soirées musicales, orch, ?early 1838, Riga, ?19 March 1838; SW xx/iii	
46b	G. Meyerbeer: cavatina 'Robert, toi que j'aime', from Robert le diable, orch transc. of harp pt, ?Nov 1838, Riga, ?30 Nov 1838; SW xx/iii	
46c	C.M. von Weber: Hunting Chorus from Euryanthe, reorchestration, ?Jan 1839, Riga, 17 Jan 1839; SW xx/iii	
62a	Various composers: suites for cornet à pistons (operatic excerpts), ?aut. 1840, lost	
62b	G. Donizetti: La favorite, various scores and arrs., ?Dec 1840–April 1841 (vs, arr. str qt, arr. 2 vn: Paris and Berlin, 1841)	
62c	H. Herz: Grande fantaisie sur La romanesca, arr. pf 4 hands, ?early 1841 (Paris, 1841)	
62d	F. Halévy: Le guitarrero, arrs., Feb–April 1841 (pf score of ov., arr. 2 vn: Paris, 1841; arr. for str/fl qt: Paris and Berlin, 1841)	
62e	F. Halévy: La reine de Chypre, arrs., probably Dec 1841–April 1842, June–July 1842 (vs, arr. str qt, arr. 2 vn: Paris and Berlin, 1842)	
62f	D.-F.-E. Auber: Zanetta, arrs. for fl qt, July 1842 (Paris, 1842–3)	
74	G. Spontini: La vestale, retouching of orch, ?Nov 1844, Dresden, 29 Nov 1844, lost	
77	C.W. Gluck: Iphigénie en Aulide, rev. of score and retouching of orch, ?Dec 1846–early Feb 1847, Dresden, 24 Feb 1847, lib (Dresden, 1847), vs (Leipzig, 1858), fs (ov. only with 1854 ending, see WWV 87 below: Leipzig, 1888); SW xx/iv	
79	G.P. da Palestrina: Stabat mater, rev. version, ?Feb–early March 1848, Dresden, 8 March 1848 (Leipzig, 1878); SW xx/ii	
83	W.A. Mozart: Don Giovanni, rev. version, early Nov 1850, Zürich, 8 Nov 1850, lost	
87	C.W. Gluck: ov. to Iphigénie en Aulide, concert ending, ?Feb–early March 1854, Zürich, 7 March 1854, fs (Leipzig, 1854), with whole ov. in Wagner's 1847 version [see WWV 77 above] (Leipzig, 1888); SW xx/iv	
109	J. Strauss: Waltz from Wein, Weib und Gesang, reorch [indicated in pf score], May 1875, ?Bayreuth, 22 May 1875, SW xx/ii	

AUTOGRAPH FACSIMILES

Der Ring des Nibelungen (Berlin, 1919) [from private print of poem, 1853]
Die Meistersinger von Nürnberg (Munich, 1922) [full score]
Tristan und Isolde (Munich, 1923) [full score]
Siegfried-Idyll (Munich, 1923) [full score]
Parsifal (Munich, 1925) [full score]
5 Gedichte für eine Frauenstimme (*Wesendonck-Lieder*) (Leipzig, 1962)
Lohengrin, preludes to Acts 1 and 3 (Leipzig, 1975) [full score]
Kinder-Katechismus zu Kosel's Geburtstag (Mainz, 1983)
Die Meistersinger von Nürnberg (lib, 1862) with essay by E. Voss (Mainz, 1983)

WRITINGS, SPEECHES

This list includes most of Wagner's writings, reviews, speeches, open letters and letters on specific subjects published in SS, as well as a number of unpublished writings; occasional poems and dedications as well as prose drafts and texts of the stage works in GS and SS are excluded, as are certain items that appeared in obscure and now inaccessible newspapers and periodicals, and items published anonymously or pseudonymously and difficult to identify.

The entries are listed in chronological order (within as well as between years) according to the date of writing. The precise form of the title, which occasionally varies from edition to edition, is taken from the Volksausgabe of the writings (Leipzig, 1911–14), except that all titles of journals and musical and literary works are rendered in italics.

Title, date	GS, SS	PW
Die deutsche Oper, 1834	xii	viii
Pasticcio, 1834	xii	viii
Eine Kritik aus Magdeburg, 1835	xvi	
Aus Magdeburg, 1836	xii	
Berliner Kunstchronik von Wilhelm Drach, 1836 [lost]		
Bellinis *Norma*, 1837 [review of perf. in Magdeburg; first pubd in F. Lippmann: 'Ein neu entdecktes Autograph Richard Wagners', *Musicae scientiae collectanea: Festschrift Karl Gustav Fellerer zum siebzigsten Geburtstag*, ed. H. Hüschen (Cologne, 1973)]		
Der dramatische Gesang, 1837	xii	
Note for the concert of 13 November 1837		
Bellini: ein Wort zu seiner Zeit, 1837	xii	viii
Theater-Anzeige, 1837 [perf. of *Norma* in Riga]	xvi	
Wagner's announcement of the concert of 19 March 1838		
Konzert-Anzeige, 1839	xvi	
Wagner's programme for the concert of 14 March 1839		
Ein Tagebuch aus Paris, 1840	xvi	
Über deutsches Musikwesen, 1840	i	vii
Über Meyerbeers *Hugenotten*, ?1840	xii	
Stabat mater de Pergolèse, arrangá … par Alexis Lvoff, 1840	xii	vii
Der Virtuos und der Künstler, 1840	i	vii
Eine Pilgerfahrt zu Beethoven, 1840	i	vii
Über die Ouvertüre, 1841	i	vii
Ein Ende in Paris, 1841	i	vii
9 Paris reports for the *Dresden Abend-Zeitung*, 1841	xii	viii
Pariser Amüsements, 1841	xii	viii
Der Künstler und die Öffentlichkeit, 1841	i	vii
Ein glücklicher Abend, 1841	i	vii
Der Freischütz: an das Pariser Publikum, 1841	i	vii
Le Freischütz in Paris: Bericht nach Deutschland, 1841	i	vii
Pariser Fatalitäten für Deutsche, 1841	xii	viii
Rossini's *Stabat mater*, 1841	i	vii
Bericht über eine neue Pariser Oper (*La reine de Chypre* von Halévy), 1841	i	vii
Ein Pariser bericht für Robert Schumanns *Neue Zeitschrift für Musik*, 1842	xvi	viii
Halévy und die französische Oper, 1842	xii	viii

Title, date	GS, SS	PW
La reine de Chypre d'Halévy, 1842	xii	
Autobiographische Skizze, 1842–3	i	i
Das Oratorium *Paulus* von Mendelssohn-Bartholdy	xii	
Zwei Schreiben an die Dresdener Liedertafel: i, Aufruf, 1843; ii, Niederlegung der Leitung, 1845	xvi	
Zwei Erklärungen über die Verdeutschung des Textes der Komposition *Les deux grenadiers*: [i], Verwahrung; [ii], Erklärung, 1843	xvi	
Rede an Webers letzter Ruhestätte, 1844 [preceded in GS by report of the reburial of Weber's remains, extracted from *Mein Leben*]	ii	vii
Die königliche Kapelle betreffend, 1846	xii	
Zu Beethovens neunter Symphonie, 1846	xii	viii
Programme note for Beethoven's Ninth Symphony, 1846 [preceded in GS by report on 1846 perf. in Dresden, extracted from *Mein Leben*]	ii	vii
Künstler und Kritiker, mit Bezug auf einen besonderen Fall, 1846	xii	viii
Eine Rede auf Friedrich Schneider, 1846	xvi	
Notes concerning the Dresden concerts of 1847–8		
Entwurf zur Organisation eines deutschen National-Theaters für das Königreich Sachsen, 1848	ii	vii
Wie verhalten sich republikanische Bestrebungen dem Königtum gegenüber, 1848	xii	iv
Vier Zeitungs-Erklärungen [i and ii from *Dresdner Anzeige*, iii from *Europe artiste*, iv from *Ostdeutsche Post*], 1848–61	xvi	
Trinkspruch am Gedenktage des 300jährigen Bestehens der königlichen musikalischen Kapelle in Dresden, 1848	ii	vii
Der Nibelungen-Mythus: als Entwurf zu einem Drama, 1848	ii	vii
Deutschland und seine Fürsten, 1848	xii	
Zwei Schreiben aus dem Jahre 1848 [i, to Franz Wigand; ii, to Lüttichau], 1848	xvi	iv
Die Wibelungen: Weltgeschichte aus der Sage, ? mid-Feb 1849, rev. 1850	ii	vii
Über Eduard Devrients *Geschichte der deutschen Schauspielkunst*, 1849	xii	viii
Theater-Reform, 1849	xii	viii
Nochmals Theater-Reform, 1849	xii	
Der Mensch und die bestehende Gesellschaft, 1849 [incl. in SS, but possibly by Röckel]	xii	viii
Die Revolution, 1849 [incl. in SS, but authorship unproven]	xii	viii
Die Kunst und die Revolution, 1849	iii	i
Flüchtige Aufzeichnung einzelner Gedanken zu einem grösseren Aufsatze: das Künstlertum der Zukunft, 1849	xii	viii
Das Kunstwerk der Zukunft, 1849	iii	i
Zu *Die Kunst und die Revolution*, 1849	xii	viii
Das Kunstwerk der Zukunft: dedication to Feuerbach, 1850	xii	
Kunst und Klima, 1850	iii	i
Vorwort zu einer 1850 beabsichtigten Herausgabe von *Siegfrieds Tod*, 1850	xvi	
Das Judentum in der Musik, 1850, rev. 1869	v	iii
Vorwort zu der 1850 beabsichtigten Veröffentlichung des Entwurfs von 1848 *Zur Organisation eines deutschen National-Theaters für Königreich Sachsen*, 1850	xvi	
Eine Skizze zu *Oper und Drama*, 1850	xvi	
Oper und Drama, 1850–51	iii, iv	ii

Title, date	GS, SS	PW
Über die musikalische Direktion der Züricher Oper, 1850	xvi	
Zur Empfehlung Gottfried Sempers, 1851	xvi	
Über die musikalische Berichterstattung in der *Eidgenössischen Zeitung*, 1851	xvi	
Beethovens *Heroische Symphonie* [programme note], 1851	v	iii
Ein Theater in Zürich, 1851	v	iii
Über die 'Goethestiftung': Brief an Franz Liszt, 1851	v	iii
Eine Mitteilung an meine Freunde, 1851	iv	i
Über musikalische Kritik: Brief an den Herausgeber der *Neuen Zeitschrift für Musik*, 1852	v	iii
Wilhelm Baumgartners Lieder, 1852	xii	
Beethovens Ouvertüre zu *Coriolan*, 1852 [programme note]	v	iii
Zum Vortrag Beethovens, 1852 [letter to Uhlig]	xvi	
Ouvertüre zu *Tannhäuser*, 1852 [programme note]	v	iii
Über die Aufführung des *Tannhäuser*: eine Mitteilung an die Dirigenten und Darsteller dieser Oper, 1852	v	iii
Vieuxtemps, 1852	xvi	
Über die Aufführung der *Tannhäuser-Ouvertüre*, 1852	xvi	
Bemerkungen zur Aufführung der Oper: *Der fliegende Holländer*, 1852	v	iii
Vorlesung der Dichtung des *Ringes des Nibelungen*, 1853 [invitation]	xvi	
Vorwort zu der Veröffentlichung der als Manuskript gedruckten Dichtung des *Ringes des Nibelungen*, 1853	xii	
Ankündigung der im Mai 1853 zu veranstaltenden Konzerte, 1853	xii	
Ouvertüre zum *Fliegenden Holländer*, 1853 [programme note]	v	iii
Zu *Tannhäuser*: i, Einzug der Gäste auf der Wartburg; ii, Tannhäusers Romfahrt, 1853 [programme notes]	xvi	
Vorspiel zu *Lohengrin*, 1853 [programme note]	v	iii
Zu *Lohengrin*: i, Männerszene und Brautzug; ii, Hochzeitsmusik und Brautlied, 1853 [programme notes]	xvi	
Über die programmatischen Erläuterungen zu den Konzerten im Mai 1853 [prefatory remarks]	xvi	
Glucks Ouvertüre zu *Iphigenia in Aulis*, 1854	v	iii
Empfehlung einer Streichquartett-Vereinigung, 1854	xvi	
Beethovens Cis moll-Quartett (Op.131), 1854 [programme note]	xii	
Dante-Schopenhauer, 1855 [letter to Liszt]	xvi	
Bemerkung zu einer angeblichen Äusserung Rossinis, 1855	xii	
Über die Leitung einer Mozart-Feier, 1856	xvi	
Über Franz Liszts Symphonische Dichtungen, 1857 [letters to Marie Sayn-Wittgenstein]	v	iii
Metaphysik der Geschlechtsliebe, 1858 [frag. letter to Schopenhauer]	xii	
Entwurf eines Amnestiegesuches an den Sächsischen Justizminister Behr, 1858	xvi	
Nachruf an L. Spohr und Chordirektor W. Fischer, 1859	v	iii
Tristan und Isolde: Vorspiel, 1859 [programme note]	xii	
Ein Brief an Hector Berlioz	vii	iii
'Zukunftsmusik': an einen französischen Freund (Fr. Villot) als Vorwort zu einer Prosa-Übersetzung meiner Operndichtungen, 1860	vii	iii
Bericht über die Aufführung des *Tannhäuser* in Paris, 1861	vii	iii
Vom Wiener Hofoperntheater, 1861	xii	

Title, date	GS, SS	PW
Gräfin Egmont ballet by Rota, 1861 [review pubd under pseud. in *Oesterreichische Zeitung*, 8 Oct 1861, and in E. Kastner: *Wagner-Catalog*, 1878]		
Drei Schreiben an die Direktion der Philharmonischen Gesellschaft in St Petersburg, 1862–6	xvi	
Vorwort zur Herausgabe der Dichtung des Bühnenfestspiels *Der Ring des Nibelungen*, 1863	vi	iii
Das Wiener Hof-Operntheater, 1863	vii	iii
Die Meistersinger von Nürnberg: Vorspiel, 1863 [programme note]	xii	
Tristan und Isolde: Vorspiel und Schluss, 1863 [programme note]	xii	
Über Staat und Religion, 1864	viii	iv
Zur Erwiderung des Aufsatzes 'Richard Wagner und die öffentliche Meinung' [by O. Redwitz], 1865	xii	
Bericht an Seine Majestät den König Ludwig II. von Bayern über eine in München zu errichtende deutsche Musikschule, 1865	viii	iv
Einladung zur ersten Aufführung von *Tristan und Isolde*, 1865 [letter to F. Uhl]	xvi	viii
Ansprache an das Hoforchester in München vor der Hauptprobe zu *Tristan und Isolde* am Vormittag des 11. Mai 1865	xvi	
Dankschreiben an das Münchener Hoforchester, 1865	xvi	
Was ist deutsch?, 1865, rev. 1878	x	iv
Ein Artikel der Münchener *Neuesten Nachrichten* vom 29. November 1865	xvi	
Mein Leben, 1865–80		
Preussen und Österreich, 1866		
Zwei Erklärungen im *Berner Bund*, 1866	xvi	
Deutsche Kunst und deutsche Politik, 1867	viii	iv
Censuren, i: W.H. Riehl: *Neues Novellenbuch*, 1867	viii	iv
Censuren, ii: Ferdinand Hiller: *Aus dem Tonleben unserer Zeit*, 1867	viii	iv
Vorwort zu der Buchausgabe der Aufsätze *Deutsche Kunst und deutsche Politik*, 1868	xvi	
Zur Widmung der zweiten Auflage von *Oper und Drama*: an Constantin Frantz, 1868	viii	ii
Zum Andante der Es dur-Symphonie von Mozart, 1868 [letter to H. von Bülow]	xvi	
Meine Erinnerungen an Ludwig Schnorr von Carolsfeld († 1865), 1868	viii	iv
Censuren, iii: Eine Erinnerung an Rossini, 1868	viii	iv
Censuren, v: Aufklärungen über *Das Judentum in der Musik* (An Frau Marie Muchanoff, geborene Gräfin Nesselrode), 1869	viii	iii
Censuren, iv: Eduard Devrient: *Meine Erinnerungen an Felix Mendelssohn-Bartholdy*, 1869	viii	iv
Vier Erklärungen in den *Signalen für die musikalische Welt*, 1869–71 [concerning, i, Hans von Bülow; ii, *Rienzi*; iii, Paris; iv, Wagner's letter to Napoleon III]	xvi	
Fragment eines Aufsatzes über Hector Berlioz, 1869	xii	
Fünf Schreiben über das Verhältnis der Kunst Richard Wagners zum Auslande, 1869–80 [i to Judith Gautier (probably written by Cosima), ii to Champfleury, iii to ed. of *American Review*, iv to Professor Gabriel Monod, v to the Duke of Bagnara (written by Cosima)]	xvi	
Zum *Judentum in der Musik* [letter to Tausig]	xvi	
Das Münchener Hoftheater: zur Berichtigung, 1869	xii	
Über das Dirigieren, 1869	viii	iv

Title, date	GS, SS	PW
Persönliches: warum ich den zahllosen Angriffen auf mich und meine Kunstansichten nichts erwidere, 1869	xii	
Die Meistersinger von Nürnberg: Vorspiel zum dritten Akt [programme note; Ger. trans. of letter to Judith Gautier], 1869	xii	
Zur Walküre: i Siegmunds Liebesgesang, ii Der Ritt der Walküren, iii Wotans Abschied und Feuerzauber, 1869 [programme notes]	xvi	
An den Wiener Hofkapellmeister Heinrich Esser, 1870	xvi	
Draft of response to Allgemeine Zeitung (unpubd), 1870 Beethoven, 1870	ix	v
Ein nicht veröffentlichter Schluss der Schrift Beethoven, 1870		
Vorwort zu Mein Leben, 1870		
Offener Brief an Dr. phil. Friedrich Stade, 1870	xvi	
Über die Bestimmung der Oper, 1871	ix	v
Rede anlässlich des Banketts im Hôtel de Rome in Berlin, 1871	ix	v
Ansprache an das Orchester in der Singakademie, 1871		
Über die Aufführung des Bühnenfestspieles: Der Ring des Nibelungen und Memorandum über Aufführung des Ring in markgräflichen Opernhaus Bayreuth, 1871		
Ankündigung der Festspiele, 1871	xvi	
Aufforderung zur Erwerbung von Patronatsscheinen, 1871	xvi	
Vorwort zu Gesamtherausgabe, 1871 [foreword to GS]	i	i
Einleitung, 1871 [introduction to vol.i of GS]	i	vii
Das Liebesverbot: Bericht über eine erste Opernaufführung, ?1871 [draws on notes for Mein Leben about perf. of 1836]	i	vii
Einleitung, 1871 [introduction to vol.ii of GS]	ii	vii
Einleitung zum dritten und vierten Bande 1871 [introduction to vols.iii and iv of GS]	iii	
Erinnerungen an Auber, 1871	ix	v
Brief an einen italienischen Freund [Boito] über die Aufführung des Lohengrin in Bologna, 1871	ix	v
Epilogischer Bericht über die Umstände und Schicksale, welche die Ausführung des Bühnenfestspiels Der Ring des Nibelungen bis zur Veröffentlichung der Dichtung desselben begleiteten, 1871	vi	iii
Ein später fortgelassener Schluss des Berichtes an den deutschen Wagner-Verein, 1871	xvi	
Rede, gehalten in Mannheim am 20. Dezember 1871		
An den Intendanten von Loën in Weimar über die Wagner-Vereine, 1871	xvi	
Eine Mitteilung an die deutschen Wagner-Vereine, 1871	xvi	
Ankündigung für den 22. Mai 1872 [laying of foundation stone in Bayreuth]	xvi	
Ankündigung der Aufführung der Neunten Symphonie für den 22. Mai 1872	xvi	
An die Patrone, 1872		
Zirkular an die Patrone über ihre Anwesenheit bei der Grundsteinlegung, 1872	xvi	
Instruction, ?1872		
Erinnerungen an Spontini, 1872 [preceded by appreciation of 1851]	v	iii
Einleitung zum fünften und sechsten Bande, 1872 [introductions to vols.v and vi of GS]	v	iii
Censuren: Vorbericht, 1872	viii	iv
Dank an die Bürger von Bayreuth nach der Grundsteinlegung am 22. Mai 1872	xvi	
Bruchstück einer Danksagung, 1872	xvi	

Title, date	GS, SS	PW
Zwei Erklärungen in der Augsburger *Allgemeinen Zeitung* über die Oper		
Theodor Körner von Wendelin Weissheimer, 1872	xvi	
An Friedrich Nietzsche, 1872	ix	v
Zwei Berichtigungen im *Musikalischen Wochenblatt*, 1872–3		
[i second report of the Academic Wagner Society, Berlin, ii Brockhaus		
Konversationslexikon]	xvi	
Über Schauspieler und Sänger, 1872	ix	v
Schrieben an den Bürgermeister von Bologna, 1872	ix	v
Über die Benennung 'Musikdrama', 1872	ix	v
Brief über das Schauspielerwesen an einen Schauspieler, 1872	ix	v
Ein Einblick in das heutige deutsche Opernwesen, 1872–3	ix	v
Zwei Reden gehalten anlässlich eines Banketts auf der Brühlschen Terrasse in		
Dresden am 14. Januar 1872		
Einleitung zu einer Vorlesung der *Götterdämmerung* vor einem ausgewählten		
Zuhörerkreise in Berlin, 1873	ix	v
An den Vorstand des Wagner-Vereins Berlin, 1873	xvi	
Zum Vortrag der neunten Symphonie Beethovens, 1873	ix	v
Das Bühnenfestspielhaus zu Bayreuth: nebst einem Bericht über die		
Grundsteinlegung desselben, 1873	ix	v
Schlussbericht über die Umstände und Schicksale, welche die Ausführung des		
Bühnenfestspieles *Der Ring des Nibelungen* bis zur Gründung von		
Wagner-Vereinen begleiteten, 1873	ix	v
An die Patrone der Bühnenfestspiele in Bayreuth, 1873 [letter of 30 August]	xii	
An die Patrone der Bühnenfestspiele in Bayreuth, 1873 [letter of 15 September]	xvi	
Zwei Erklärungen (i Notgedrungene Erklärung, ii Die 'Presse' zu den		
'Proben'), 1874, 1875	xii	
Über eine Opernaufführung in Leipzig: Brief an den Herausgeber des		
Musikalischen Wochenblattes, 1874	x	vi
Einladungs-Schreiben an die Sänger für Proben und Aufführungen des		
Bühnenfestspiels *Der Ring des Nibelungen*, 1875	xvi	
An die Orchester-Mitglieder, 1875	xvi	
Zur *Götterdämmerung*: i Vorspiel, ii Hagens Wacht, iii Siegfrieds Tod, iv		
Schluss des letzten Aktes, 1875 [programme notes]	xvi	
Ankündigung der Festspiele für 1876, 1875	xvi	
Über Bewerbungen zu den Festspielen, 1875	xvi	
An die Künstler, 1875	xvi	
Austeilung der Rollen, 1875		
Voranschlag der 'Entschädigungen', 1876		
Skizzierung der Proben und Aufführungen 1876, 1876		
An die Orchestermitglieder (Einladung), 1876	xvi	
An die Sänger (Einladung), 1876	xvi	
Für die Patrone, 1876	xvi	
An die Ehrenpatrone, 1876		
Verzeichnis der Ehrenpatrone und Freikarten Empfänger, 1876		
Circular, die 'Costümproben auf der beleuchteten Bühne' betreffend, 1876		
Anordnung der Proben zu den Aufführungen des Bühnenfestspieles *Der*		
Ring des Nibelungen in Bayreuth im Jahre 1876		
Über den Gebrauch des Textbuches, 1876	xvi	

Title, date	GS, SS	PW
Über den Hervorruf, 1876	xvi	
Für das Orchester, 1876	xvi	
Letzte Bitte an meine lieben Genossen! Letzter Wunsch, 1876	xvi	
Ansprache nach Schluss der *Götterdämmerung*, 1876 [authenticity uncertain]	xvi	
Abschiedswort an die Künstler, 1876 [authenticity uncertain]	xvi	
Gedanken über Zahlung des Defizits und Fortführung der Festspiele, 1876	xvi	
An die geehrten Patrone der Bühnenfestspiele von 1876, 1876	xii	
Entwürfe und Notizen zu den Programmen der (1.) 6 Konzerte in London, 1877		
Entwurf: veröffentlicht mit den Statuten des Patronatvereines, 1877 [proposal of music school for Bayreuth]	x	vi
Ansprache an die Abgesandten des Bayreuther Patronats, 1877	xii	
Aufforderung zur Anmeldung für die Stilbildungsschule, 1877		
Ankündigung der Aufführung des *Parsifal*, 1877	xii	vi
Zur Einführung (*Bayreuther Blätter*, erstes Stück), 1878	x	vi
An die geehrten Vorstände der noch bestehenden lokalen Wagner-Vereine, 1878	xvi	
Modern, 1878	x	vi
Erläuterung des *Siegfried Idylls* für S.M. den König, 1878		
Publikum und Popularität, 1878	x	vi
Das Publikum in Zeit und Raum, 1878	x	vi
Ein Rückblick auf die Bühnenfestspiele des Jahres 1876, 1878	x	vi
Metaphysik. Kunst und Religion. Moral. Christentum [frags.], 1878–82	xii	viii
Ein Wort zur Einführung der Arbeit Hans von Wolzogens *Über Verrottung und Errettung der deutschen Sprache*, 1879	x	vi
Wollen wir hoffen?, 1879	x	vi
Über das Dichten und Komponieren, 1879	x	vi
Erklärung an die Mitglieder des Patronatvereines, 1879	x	vi
Über das Operndichten und Komponieren im Besonderen, 1879	x	vi
Über die Anwendung der Musik auf das Drama, 1879	x	vi
Offenes Schreiben an Herrn Ernst von Weber, Verfasser der Schrift: *Die Folterkammern der Wissenschaft*, 1879	x	vi
Zur Einführung in das Jahr 1880, 1879	x	vi
Religion und Kunst, 1880	x	vi
An König Ludwig II. über die Aufführung des *Parsifal*, 1880	xvi	
'Was nützt diese Erkenntnis?': ein Nachtrag zu: *Religion und Kunst*, 1880	x	vi
Parsifal: Vorspiel, 1880 [programme note]	xii	viii
Zur Mitteilung an die geehrten Patrone der Bühnenfestspiele in Bayreuth, 1880	x	vi
Gedanken zur Fortführung der Festspiele, 1880		
Ausführungen zu *Religion und Kunst*: i 'Erkenne dich selbst', ii Heldentum und Christentum, 1881	x	vi
Zur Einführung der Arbeit des Grafen Gobineau: *Ein Urteil über die jetzige Weltlage*	x	vi
Einladung der Sänger, 1882		
Austeilung der Partien, 1882		
Begleitschreiben zur 'Austeilung' der Partien sowie Plan der Proben und Aufführungen, 1882		

Title, date	GS, SS	PW
Sketch of rehearsal plan, 1882		
Brief an H. v. Wolzogen, 1882	x	vi
Offenes Schreiben an Herrn Friedrich Schön in Worms, 1882	x	vi
Rede, gehalten in Wahnfried anlässlich der Hochzeit Blandine von Bülows, 1882		
Danksagung an die Bayreuther Bürgerschaft, 1882	xvi	
Das Bühnenweihfestspiel in Bayreuth 1882, 1882	x	vi
Bericht über die Wiederaufführung eines Jugendwerkes: an den Herausgeber des *Musikalischen Wochenblattes*, 1882	x	vi
Brief an H. v. Stein, 1883	x	vi
Über das Weibliche im Menschlichen [inc.], 1883	xii	vi

BIBLIOGRAPHY

A: Anthologies, other editions. B: Catalogues, bibliographies, related studies. C: Iconographical studies. D: Correspondence. E: Periodicals. F: Contemporary essays. G: Personal accounts, reminiscences. H: Principal biographies. I: Other biographical and related studies. J: Bayreuth: the Festspielhaus, its politics and influence. K: Production studies. L: Literary and philosophical studies. M: Analysis and criticism: general studies. N: Analysis and criticism: individual studies. O: Wagnerism.

A: Anthologies, other Editions

C.F. Glasenapp and H. von Stein: *Wagner-Lexikon: Hauptbegriffe der Kunst- und Weltanschauung Richard Wagners in wörtlichen Anführungen aus seinen Schriften* (Stuttgart, 1883)

C.F. Glasenapp: *Wagner-Encyklopädie: Haupterscheinungen der Kunst- und Kulturgeschichte im Lichte der Anschauung Richard Wagners* (Leipzig, 1891/R)

J. Kapp, ed.: *Der junge Wagner: Dichtungen, Aufsätze, Entwürfe 1832–1849* (Berlin, 1910)

W. Golther, ed.: *Richard Wagner: Gesammelte Schriften und Dichtungen in zehn Bänden* (Berlin, 1913) [incl. prefatory life and works, suppl. vol. of notes and commentary]

A. Lorenz, ed.: *Richard Wagner: ausgewählte Schriften und Briefe* (Berlin, 1938)

M. Gregor-Dellin, ed.: *Richard Wagner: Mein Leben* (Munich, 1963, 2/1976; Eng. trans., Cambridge, 1983) [1st authentic edn]

A. Goldman and E. Sprinchorn, eds.: *Wagner on Music and Drama: a Compendium of Richard Wagner's Prose Works* (New York, 1964/R) [trans. W.A. Ellis]

G. Strobel and W. Wolf, eds.: 'Die rote Brieftasche', *Richard Wagner: Sämtliche Briefe*, i (Leipzig, 1967), 81–92 [autobiographical notes for 1813–39]

C. Dahlhaus, ed.: *Wagners Ästhetik* (Bayreuth, 1972; Eng. trans., Bayreuth, 1972)

R.L. Jacobs and G. Skelton, eds. and trans.: *Wagner Writes from Paris: Stories, Essays and Articles by the Young Composer* (London and New York, 1973)

C. Osborne, ed.: *Richard Wagner: Stories and Essays* (London, 1973) [rev. of Eng. trans. by W.A. Ellis]

D. Mack, ed.: *Ausgewählte Schriften* (Frankfurt, 1974) [incl. essay by Ernst Bloch]

J. Bergfeld, ed.: *Das braune Buch: Tagebuchaufzeichnungen 1865–1882* (Zürich and Freiburg, 1975; Eng. trans., London, 1980) [incl. frags., sketches and the 'annals' (autobiographical notes for 1846–68)]

E. Voss, ed.: *Schriften eines revolutionären Genies* (Munich, 1976)

M. Gregor-Dellin and D. Mack, eds.: *Cosima Wagner: die Tagebücher 1869–1883* (Munich, 1976–7; Eng. trans., London and New York, 1978–80)

E. Voss, ed.: *Schriften: ein Schlüssel zu Leben, Werk und Zeit* (Frankfurt, 1978)

R. Jacobs, ed. and trans.: *Three Wagner Essays* (London, 1979)

M. Gregor-Dellin, ed.: *Mein Denken* (Munich, 1982)

D. Borchmeyer, ed.: *Dichtungen und Schriften* (Frankfurt, 1983)

K. Kropfinger, ed.: *Richard Wagner: Oper und Drama* (Stuttgart, 1984)

B: Catalogues, bibliographies, related studies

E. Kastner: *Wagner-Catalog: chronologisches Verzeichniss der von und über Richard Wagner erschienenen Schriften, Musikwerke etc.* (Offenbach, 1878/R)

N. Oesterlein: *Katalog einer Richard Wagner-Bibliothek: nach den vorliegenden Originalien zu einem authentischen Nachschlagebuch durch die gesammte, insbesondere deutsche Wagner-Litteratur bearbeitet und veröffentlicht* (Leipzig, 1882–95)

H. Silège: *Bibliographie wagnérienne française* (Paris, 1902)

Catalogue of the Burrell Collection (London, 1929)

O. Strobel: *Genie am Werk: Richard Wagners Schaffen und Wirken im Spiegel eigenhandschriftlicher Urkunden: Führer durch die einmalige Ausstellung einer umfassenden Auswahl von Schätzen aus dem Archiv des Hauses Wahnfried* (Bayreuth, 1933, 2/1934)

E.M. Terry: *A Richard Wagner Dictionary* (New York, 1939/R)

O. Strobel: 'Richard-Wagner-Forschungsstätte und Archiv des Hauses Wahnfried', *Das Bayernland*, lii (1942), 457–66; repr. in *Bayreuth: die Stadt Richard Wagners*, ed. O. Strobel and L. Deubner (Munich, 2/1943), 39–47

H. Barth, ed.: *Internationale Wagner-Bibliographie: 1945–55* (Bayreuth, 1956); *1956–60* (1961); *1961–6* (1968); *1967–78* (1979)

H.-M. Plesske: *Richard Wagner in der Dichtung: Bibliographie deutschsprachiger Veröffentlichungen* (Bayreuth, 1971)

H.F.G. Klein *Erst- und Frühdrucke der Textbücher von Richard Wagner: Bibliographie* (Tutzing, 1979)

G. Bott, ed.: *Die Meistersinger und Richard Wagner: die Rezeptionsgeschichte einer Oper von 1868 bis heute* (Nuremberg, 1981) [Germanisches National-museum exhibition catalogue]

H.F.G. Klein: *Erstdrucke der musikalischen Werke von Richard Wagner: Bibliographie* (Tutzing, 1983)

Richard Wagner und die politischen Bewegungen seiner Zeit (Koblenz, 1983) [Bundesarchiv exhibition catalogue]

M. Eger, ed.: *Wagner und die Juden: Fakten und Hintergründe* (Bayreuth, 1985) [documentation accompanying exhibition in the Richard-Wagner-Museum, Bayreuth]

J. Deathridge, M. Geck and E. Voss: *Wagner Werk-Verzeichnis (WWV): Verzeichnis der musikalischen Werke Richard Wagners und ihrer Quellen* (Mainz, 1986)

S. Spencer: 'The Stefan Zweig Collection' [incl. annotated list of Wagner MSS], *Wagner*, viii (1987), 4–13

E. Voss: 'Von Notwendigkeit und Nutzen der Wagnerforschung: ein Abriss über das Wagner-Werk-Verzeichnis und die Wagner-Gesamtausgaben', *Bayreuther Festspiele: Programmheft I. Lohengrin* (Bayreuth, 1987), 16–41 [incl. Eng. trans.]

C: Iconographical studies

E. Kreowski and E. Fuchs: *Richard Wagner in der Karikatur* (Berlin, 1907)

E.W. Engel: *Richard Wagners Leben und Werke im Bilde* (Leipzig, 1913)

R. Bory: *La vie et l'oeuvre de Richard Wagner par l'image* (Lausanne, 1938)

W. Schuh: *Renoir und Wagner* (Zürich, 1959)

M.E. Tralbaut: *Richard Wagner im Blickwinkel fünf grosser Maler* (Dortmund, 1965)

M. Geck: *Die Bildnisse Richard Wagners* (Munich, 1970)

H. Barth, D. Mack and E. Voss: *Wagner: sein Leben, sein Werk und seine Welt in zeitgenössischen Bildern und Texten* (Vienna, 1975, 2/1982; Eng. trans., 1975)

M. Gregor-Dellin: *Richard Wagner: eine Biographie in Bildern* (Munich, 1982)

E. Drusche: *Richard Wagner* (Wiesbaden, 1983)

D: Correspondence

Catalogues, anthologies, collected editions

W. Altmann: *Richard Wagners Briefe nach Zeitfolge und Inhalt: ein Beitrag zur Lebensgeschichte des Meisters* (Leipzig, 1905/R)

Helbing auction catalogue, Munich, 11 May 1909 [25 autograph letters from collection of Hofrat Edgar Hanfstaengl]

J.N. Burk, ed.: *Letters of Richard Wagner: the Burrell Collection* (New York, 1950/R)

G. Strobel, W. Brieg and others, eds.: *Richard Wagner: Sämtliche Briefe* (Leipzig, Wiesbaden and Paris, 1967–)

Musikantiquariat Hans Schneider catalogues 215 [Richard Wagner, ii: Documents, 1850–64], 222 ['Gruss an die Schweiz', Zürich antiquarian fair], 223 [Richard Wagner, iii: Documents, 1865–83] (Tutzing, 1978)

D. Mack, ed.: *Cosima Wagner: das zweite Leben: Briefe und Aufzeichnungen 1883–1930* (Munich, 1980)

H. Kesting, ed.: *Richard Wagner: Briefe* (Munich, 1983) [annotated edn of 206 letters]

W. Otto, ed.: *Richard Wagner: Briefe 1830–1883* (Berlin, 1986) [annotated edn of 402 letters]

S. Spencer and B. Millington, eds.: *Selected Letters of Richard Wagner* (London, 1987) [Eng. trans. of 500 letters, with orig. texts of passages omitted from existing printed edns]

H. Kesting, ed.: *Franz Liszt – Richard Wagner: Briefwechsel* (Frankfurt, 1988)

W. Breig, M. Dürrer and A. Mielke, eds.: *Chronologisches Verzeichnis der Briefe von Richard Wagner* (Wiesbaden, 1998)

Individual publications

Bisher ungedruckte Briefe von Richard Wagner an Ernst von Weber (Dresden, 1883) [several Wagner letters 1879–81]

F. Hueffer, ed.: *Briefwechsel zwischen Wagner und Liszt* (Leipzig, 1887, 2/1900, enlarged E. Kloss, 3/1910, 4/1919; Eng. trans., 1888, rev. 2/1897/R by W.A. Ellis)

E. Wille: *Fünfzehn Briefe von Richard Wagner, nebst Erinnerungen und Erläuterungen* (Leipzig, 1887, 2/1908 by W. Golther, 3/1935 by C.F. Meyer)

H. von Wolzogen, ed.: *Richard Wagner's Briefe an Theodor Uhlig, Wilhelm Fischer, Ferdinand Heine* (Leipzig, 1888; Eng. trans., 1890) [see also O. Strobel: 'Unbekannte Lebensdokumente Richard Wagners: 2 unveröffentlichte Briefe Wagners an Theodor Uhlig', *Die Sonne*, x (1933), 69–77, and J.N. Burk, ed.: *Letters of Richard Wagner: the Burrell Collection* (New York, 1950/R), 607–41]

H.S. Chamberlain, ed.: *Richard Wagners echte Briefe an Ferdinand Praeger* (Bayreuth, 1894, 2/1908)

La Mara [M. Lipsius], ed.: *Briefe an August Röckel von Richard Wagner* (Leipzig, 1894, 2/1912; Eng. trans., 1897)

J. Hoffmann, ed.: *Richard und Cosima Wagner an Maler Josef Hoffmann* (Bayreuth, 1896) [letters in facs.]

E. Kastner, ed.: *Briefe von Richard Wagner an seine Zeitgenossen* (Berlin, 1897)

A. Heintz, ed.: *Briefe Richard Wagner's an Otto Wesendonck* (Charlottenburg, 1898, enlarged 2/1905 by W. Golther; Eng. trans., 1911/R)

K. Heckel, ed.: *Briefe Richard Wagners an Emil Heckel: zur Entstehungsgeschichte der Bühnenfestspiele in Bayreuth* (Berlin, 1899, 3/1911; Eng. trans., 1899)

W. Golther, ed.: *Richard Wagner an Mathilde Wesendonck: Tagebuchblätter und Briefe 1853–1871* (Leipzig, 1904, 44/1914; Eng. trans., 1905/R) [see also J. Kapp: 'Unterdrückte Dokumente aus den Briefen Richard Wagners an Mathilde Wesendonck', *Die Musik*, xxiii (1930–31), 877–83, and O. Strobel: 'Über einen unbekannten Brief Richard Wagners an Mathilde Wesendonck und seine Geschichte', *Bayreuther Festspielführer 1937*, 152–8]

D. Spitzer, ed.: *Briefe Richard Wagners an eine Putzmacherin* (Vienna, 1906, enlarged 2/1967 by L. Kusche; Eng. trans., 1941)

C.F. Glasenapp, ed.: *Bayreuther Briefe von Richard Wagner (1871–1883)* (Berlin, 1907, 2/1907–8/R; Eng. trans., 1912, as *The Story of Bayreuth*)

C.F. Glasenapp, ed.: *Familienbriefe von Richard Wagner 1832–1874* (Berlin, 1907; Eng. trans., 1911, enlarged 1991 by J. Deathridge)

E. Kloss, ed.: *Richard Wagner an seine Künstler* (Berlin, 1908)

H. von Wolzogen, ed.: *Richard Wagner an Minna Wagner* (Berlin, 1908; Eng. trans., 1909)

E. Kloss, ed.: *Richard Wagner an Freunde und Zeitgenossen* (Berlin, 1909)

T. Apel, ed.: *Richard Wagner an Theodor Apel* (Leipzig, 1910)

W. Altmann, ed.: *Richard Wagners Briefwechsel mit seinen Verlegern*, i: *Briefwechsel mit Breitkopf & Härtel* (Leipzig, 1911); ii: *Briefwechsel mit B. Schott's Söhne* (Mainz, 1911)

S. Röckl: 'Zwei unbekannte Briefe Richard Wagners an Heinrich Vogl', *Rheinische Musik- u. Theater-Zeitung*, xii/51–2 (1911), 706–7

M. Huch, ed.: 'Drei unbekannte Schreiben Richard Wagners an Gustav Hölzel', *Die Musik*, xii/3 (1912–13), 171–2

L. Schemann: *Quellen und Untersuchungen zum Leben Gobineaus*, i (Strasbourg, 1914), ii (Berlin and Leipzig, 1919)

E. Förster-Nietzsche: *Wagner und Nietzsche zur Zeit ihrer Freundschaft: Erinnerungsgabe zu Friedrich Nietzsches 70. Geburtstag den 15. Oktober 1914* (Munich, 1915; Eng. trans., 1921/R as *The Nietzsche–Wagner Correspondence*)

J.G. Prod'homme: 'Wagner and the Paris Opéra: Unpublished Letters (February–March, 1861)', *MQ*, i (1915), 216–31

D. Thode, ed.: *Richard Wagners Briefe an Hans von Bülow* (Jena, 1916)

S. von Hausegger, ed.: *Richard Wagners Briefe an Frau Julie Ritter* (Munich, 1920)

'Lettres inédites de Wagner à Léon Leroy et Gaspérini', *ReM*, iv/11 (1923), 139–48

W. Altmann, ed.: 'Briefe Wagners an Editha von Rhaden', *Die Musik*, xvi (1923–4), 712–32

W. Altmann, ed.: *Richard Wagner und Albert Niemann: ein Gedenkbuch mit bisher unveröffentlichten Briefen* (Berlin, 1924)

L. Karpath, ed.: *Richard Wagner: Briefe an Hans Richter* (Berlin, 1924)

R. Sternfeld: 'Richard Wagner in seinen Briefen an "Das Kind"', *Die Musik*, xix (1926–7), 1–11

H. Scholz, ed.: *Richard Wagner an Mathilde Maier (1862–1878)* (Leipzig, 1930)

H.J. Moser: 'Zwanzig Richard-Wagner-Dokumente', *Deutsche Rundschau*, Jg.57 (1931), 42–54, 133–49

E. Lenrow, ed. and trans.: *The Letters of Richard Wagner to Anton Pusinelli* (New York, 1932/R)

G. Kinsky, ed.: 'Fünf ungedruckte Briefe Wagners an Meyerbeer', *SMz*, lxxiv (1934), 705–16

J. Tiersot, ed.: *Lettres françaises de Richard Wagner* (Paris, 1935)

W. Schuh, ed. and trans.: *Die Briefe Richard Wagners an Judith Gautier* (Zürich, 1936, enlarged, with Fr. orig., 1964 as *Richard et Cosima Wagner: lettres à Judith Gautier*, ed. L. Guichard)

O. Strobel, ed.: *König Ludwig II. und Richard Wagner: Briefwechsel*: Briefwechsel, v: *Neue Urfunden zur Lebensgeschichte Richard Wagners 1864–1882* (Karlsruhe, 1936–9)

W. Jerger, ed.: *Wagner-Nietzsches Briefwechsel während des Tribschener Idylls* (Berne, 1951)

L. Strecker: *Richard Wagner als Verlagsgefährte: eine Darstellung mit Briefen und Dokumenten* (Mainz, 1951)

A. Zinsstag, ed.: *Zur Erinnerung an Malwida von Meysenbug* (Basle, 1956) [contains 9 previously unpubd Wagner letters]

A. Zinsstag: *Die Briefsammlungen des Richard-Wagner-Museums in Tribschen bei Luzern* (Basle, 1961)

W. Grupe: 'Wagner-Briefe im Deutschen Zentralarchiv, Abteilung Merseburg', *Musikund Gesellschaft*, xiv (1964), 682–4

H. Oesterheld: 'Dokumente zur Musikgeschichte Meiningens', *Neue Beiträge zur Regerforschung und Musikgeschichte Meiningens*, Südthüringer Forschung, vi (1970) [5 letters to Duke Georg II of Saxe-Meiningen and his wife]

D. Petzet and M. Petzet: *Die Richard Wagner-Bühne König Ludwigs II.* (Munich, 1970) [contains previously unpubd correspondence with Düfflipp]

U. Sautter and H.E. Onnau: *Constantin Frantz: Briefe* (Wiesbaden, 1974)

G. Colli and M. Montinari, eds.: *Nietzsche: Briefwechsel* (Berlin, 1975–84)

K. Liepmann: 'Wagner's Proposal to America', *HiFi*, xxv/12 (1975), 70–72

R.P. Locke: *Fenway Court: Annual Report of the Isabella Stewart Gardner Museum* (Boston, 1975) [letters from Bayreuth]

W. Keller, ed.: *Richard Wagner: Briefe an Wilhelm Baumgartner 1850–1861* (Zürich, 1976)

E. Voss: 'Wagners "Sämtliche Briefe"?', *Melos/NZM*, iv (1978), 219–23

J. Deathridge: 'Wagner und sein erster Lehrmeister: mit einem unveröffentlichten Brief Richard Wagners', *Bayerische Staatsoper: Programmheft zur Neuinszenierung Die Meistersinger von Nürnberg* (Munich, 1979), 71–5

J. Deathridge: 'Wagner und Spontini: mit einem unveröffentlichten Brief Richard Wagners', *Jb der Bayerischen Staatsoper* (1979), 68–76

M. Eger: 'Der Briefwechsel Richard und Cosima Wagner: Geschichte und Relikte einer vernichteten Korrespondenz', *Bayreuther Festspiele: Programmheft IV. Das Rheingold* (Bayreuth, 1979), 1–23, 108–19; *Programmheft V. Die Walküre* (Bayreuth, 1979), 1–23, 108–32 [incl. Eng. trans.]

S. Kohler: '"Die Welt ist mir einmal durchaus conträr!" Richard Wagner und Malwida von Meysenburg: Geschichte einer Freundschaft', *Jb der Bayerischen Staatsoper* (Munich, 1981), 61–101

S. Spencer: 'Wagner Autographs in London', *Wagner*, iv (1983), 98–114; v (1984), 2–20, 45–52 [24 previously unpubd letters, with Eng. trans., from the *GB-Lbl* collection]

O. Pausch: 'Ein Brief Richard Wagners an Peter Cornelius über "Eine kuriose Geldangelegenheit" ', *Richard Wagner: Salzburg 1983*, 541–7

J. Marshall: 'Richard Wagner's Letter to Australia', *The Richard Wagner Centenary in Australia*, ed. P. Dennison (Adelaide, 1985), 149–65

B. Millington: 'The "Kaisermarsch" in Leipzig: an Unpublished Wagner Letter', *Wagner*, viii (1987), 2–4

E. Periodicals

Bayreuther Blätter, i–lxi (1878–1938)

Revue wagnérienne, i–iii (1885–8)

The Meister: the Quarterly Journal of the London Branch of the Wagner Society, i–viii (1885–95)

Richard Wagner-Jb, i (1886)

Richard Wagner-Jb, i–v (1906–8, 1912–13)

Tribschener Blätter: Mitteilungen der Gesellschaft Richard Wagner-Museum Tribschen (Lucerne, 1956–)

Feuilles Wagnériennes: bulletin d' information de l'association Wagnérienne de Belgique (Brussels, 1960–)

Wagner (new ser.), ed. S. Spencer (London, 1980–)

F: Contemporary essays

F. Liszt: *Lohengrin et Tannhäuser de Richard Wagner* (Leipzig, 1851)

J. Raff: *Die Wagnerfrage: kritisch beleuchtet*, i: *Wagners letzte künstlerische Kundgebung im 'Lohengrin'* (Brunswick, 1854) [no more pubd]

F. Liszt: 'Richard Wagner's Rheingold', *NZM*, xliv (1855), 1–3

H. von Bülow: *Über Richard Wagner's Faust-Ouvertüre: eine erläuternde Mittheilung an die Dirigenten, Spieler und Hörer dieses Werkes* (Leipzig, 1860)

Champfleury [H. Husson]: *Richard Wagner* (Paris, 1860)

C. Baudelaire: *Richard Wagner et Tannhäuser à Paris* (Paris, 1861/R; Eng. trans., 1964) [orig. pubd in *Revue européenne* (1 April 1861); monograph incl. new section]

F. Nietzsche: *Die Geburt der Tragödie aus dem Geiste der Musik* (Leipzig, 1872, enlarged 3/1886; Eng. trans., 1967)

H. Porges: *Die Aufführung von Beethovens Neunter Symphonie unter Richard Wagner in Bayreuth* (Leipzig, 1872)

E. Dannreuther: *Richard Wagner: his Tendencies and Theories* (London, 1873)

E. Hanslick: *Die Moderne Oper* (Berlin, 1875)

E. Schuré: *Le drame musical*, ii: *Richard Wagner: son oeuvre et son idée* (Paris, 1875, 4/1895; Eng. trans., 1910)

W. Mohr: *Richard Wagner und das Kunstwerk der Zukunft im Lichte der Bayreuther Aufführung betrachtet* (Cologne, 1876)

C.F. Glasenapp: *Richard Wagner's Leben und Wirken* (Kassel, 1876–7) [see 'Principal biographies']

M. Plüddemann: *Die Bühnenfestspiele in Bayreuth* (Colberg, 1877, 2/1881)

F. von Hausegger: *Richard Wagner und Schopenhauer* (Leipzig, 1878, 2/1892)

H. Porges: *Die Bühnenproben zu den Bayreuther Festspielen des Jahres 1876* (Chemnitz and Leipzig, 1881–96/R; Eng. trans., 1983)

J. Gautier: *Richard Wagner et son oeuvre poétique depuis Rienzi jusqu'à Parsifal* (Paris, 1882)

R. Pohl: *Gesammelte Schriften über Musik und Musiker*, i: *Richard Wagner* (Leipzig, 1883)

G: Personal accounts, reminiscences

H. Dorn: *Aus meinem Leben* (Berlin, 1870)

M. von Meysenbug: *Memoiren einer Idealistin* (Berlin, ?1875; Eng. trans., 1937)

F. Nietzsche: *Unzeitgemässe Betrachtungen*, iv: *Richard Wagner in Bayreuth* (Chemnitz, 1876; Eng. trans., 1910)

H. Dorn: *Ergebnisse aus Erlebnissen* (Berlin, 1877)

R. Pohl: 'Richard Wagner', *Sammlung musikalischer Vorträge*, v/53–4, ed. P. Waldersee (Leipzig, 1883), 123–98

H. von Wolzogen: *Erinnerungen an Richard Wagner* (Vienna, 1883, enlarged 2/1891; Eng. trans., 1894)

C. Mendès: *Richard Wagner* (Paris, 1886)

K. Heckel: *Die Bühnenfestspiele in Bayreuth* (Leipzig, 1891)

F. Weingartner: *Bayreuth (1876–1896)* (Leipzig, 1896, 2/1904)

A. Lavignac: *Le voyage artistique à Bayreuth* (Paris, 1897, rev. 1951 by H. Busser; Eng. trans., 1898, as *The Music Dramas of Richard Wagner*, 2/1904/R)

W. Weissheimer: *Erlebnisse mit Richard Wagner, Franz Liszt und vielen anderen Zeitgenossen nebst deren Briefen* (Stuttgart, 1898)

E. Schuré: *Souvenirs sur Richard Wagner: la première de 'Tristan et Iseult'* (Paris, 1900)

L. Schemann: *Meine Erinnerungen an Richard Wagner* (Stuttgart, 1902)

M. Kietz: *Richard Wagner in den Jahren 1842–1849 und 1873–1875: Erinnerungen von Gustav Adolph Kietz* (Dresden, 1905)

H. Zumpe: *Persönliche Erinnerungen nebst Mitteilungen aus seinen Tagebuchblättern und Briefen* (Munich, 1905)

R. Fricke: *Bayreuth vor dreissig Jahren: Erinnerungen an Wahnfried und aus dem Festspielhause* (Dresden, 1906); Eng. trans. in *Wagner*, xi (1990), 93–109, 134–50, and xii (1991), 3–24 [diary kept by production assistant at first Bayreuth Festival]

E. Michotte: *La visite de Richard Wagner à Rossini (Paris, 1860)* (Paris, 1906; Eng. trans., 1968)

E. Humperdinck: 'Parsifal-Skizzen: persönliche Erinnerungen an R. Wagner und an die erste Aufführung des Bühnenweihfestspieles am 25. Juli 1882', *Die Zeit* (Vienna, 1907); pubd separately (Siegburg, 1949)

A. Neumann: *Erinnerungen an Richard Wagner* (Leipzig, 1907; Eng. trans., 1908/R)

J. Gautier *Le collier des jours: souvenirs de ma vie*, iii (Paris, 1909; rev. edn in *Mercure de France*, 1943; Eng. trans., 1910)

H. Schmidt and U. Hartmann, eds.: *Richard Wagner in Erinnerungen* (Leipzig, 1909)

J. Hey: *Richard Wagner als Vortragsmeister: Erinnerungen*, ed. H. Hey (Leipzig, 1911)

L. Frankenstein, ed.: *Theodor Uhlig: musikalische Schriften* (Regensburg, 1913)

M. Fehr: *Unter Wagners Taktstock: Dreissig Winterthurer- und Zürcherbriefe aus der Zeit der Wagnerkonzerte in Zürich 1852* (Winterthur, 1922)

S. Wagner: *Erinnerungen* (Stuttgart, 1923, enlarged 2/1935)

F. Klose: *Bayreuth: Eindrücke und Erlebnisse* (Regensburg, 1929)

E. Thierbach, ed.: *Die Briefe Cosima Wagners an Friedrich Nietzsche* (Weimar, 1938–40)

W. Krienitz: 'Felix Mottls Tagebuchaufzeichnungen aus den Jahren 1873–1876', *Neue Wagner Forschungen*, ed. O. Strobel, i (Karlsruhe, 1943), 167–234

P. Cook, ed.: *A Memoir of Bayreuth: 1876* (London, 1979) [Carl Emil Doepler's account of the first Bayreuth Festival; incl. his costume designs]

H: Principal biographies

C.F. Glasenapp: *Richard Wagner's Leben und Wirken* (Kassel, 1876–7, enlarged 3/1894–1911 as *Das Leben Richard Wagners*, 5/1910–23; Eng. trans. of 3rd edn, enlarged 1900–08/*R* by W.A. Ellis as *Life of Richard Wagner* [vols. iv–vi by Ellis alone])

M. Burrell: *Richard Wagner: his Life & Works from 1813 to 1834* (London, 1898)

M. Koch: *Richard Wagner* (Berlin, 1907–18)

E. Newman: *The Life of Richard Wagner* (London, 1933–47/*R*)

M. Fehr: *Richard Wagners Schweizer Zeit*, i [1849–55] (Aarau and Leipzig, 1934); ii [1855–72, 1883] (Aarau and Frankfurt, 1953)

C. von Westernhagen: *Richard Wagner: sein Werk, sein Wesen, seine Welt* (Zürich, 1956)

R.W. Gutman: *Richard Wagner: the Man, his Mind, and his Music* (New York and London, 1968)

C. von Westernhagen: *Wagner* (Zürich, 1968, enlarged 2/1978; Eng. trans., 1978)

J. Chancellor: *Wagner* (London, 1978)

R. Taylor: *Richard Wagner: his Life, Art and Thought* (London, 1979)

D. Watson: *Richard Wagner: a Biography* (London, 1979)

M. Gregor-Dellin: *Richard Wagner: sein Leben, sein Werk, sein Jahrhundert* (Munich, 1980, 2/1983; Eng. trans., abridged, 1983)

J. Deathridge and C. Dahlhaus: *The New Grove Wagner* (London, 1984)

B. Millington: *Wagner* (London, 1984, 2/1992)

I: Other biographical and related studies

F. Hueffer: *Richard Wagner* (London, 1872, 3/1912)

A. Jullien: *Richard Wagner: sa vie et ses oeuvres* (Paris, 1886; Eng. trans., 1892/*R*)

H.S. Chamberlain: *Richard Wagner* (Munich, 1896, 9/1936; Eng. trans., 1897/*R*)

W. Kienzl: *Die Gesamtkunst des XIX. Jahrhunderts: Richard Wagner* (Munich, 1904, 2/1908)

M. Semper: *Das Münchener Festspielhaus: Gottfried Semper und Richard Wagner* (Hamburg, 1906)

C. von Ehrenfels: *Richard Wagner und seine Apostaten* (Vienna, 1913)

E. Newman: *Wagner as Man and Artist* (London, 1914, 2/1924/*R*)

W. Lippert: *Richard Wagner's Verbannung und Rückkehr 1849–1862* (Dresden, 1927; Eng. trans., 1930, as *Wagner in Exile*)

J. Kniese, ed.: *Der Kampf zweier Welten um das Bayreuther Erbe: Julius Knieses Tagebuchblätter aus dem Jahre 1883* (Leipzig, 1931)

E. Newman: *Fact and Fiction about Wagner* (London, 1931)

G. de Pourtalès: *Wagner: histoire d'un artiste* (Paris, 1932, enlarged 2/1942; Eng. trans., 1932/*R*)

K. Geiringer: 'Wagner and Brahms, with Unpublished Letters', *MQ*, xxii (1936), 178–89

W. Reihlen: 'Die Stammtafel Richard Wagners (Leipziger Abschnitt)', *Familiengeschichtliche Blätter*, xxxviii (1940), 170

W. Reihlen: 'Die Eltern Richard Wagners', *Familiengeschichtliche Blätter*, xli (1943), 41

O. Strobel, ed.: *Neue Wagner-Forschungen* (Karlsruhe, 1943)

W. Rauschenberger: 'Die Abstammung Richard Wagners', *Familiengeschichtliche Blätter*, xlii (1944), 9

O. Strobel: *Richard Wagner: Leben und Schaffen: eine Zeittafel* (Bayreuth, 1952)

H. Mayer: *Richard Wagners geistige Entwicklung* (Düsseldorf, 1954)

H. Engel: 'Wagner und Spontini', *AMw*, xii (1955), 167–77

W. Vordtriede: 'Richard Wagners "Tod in Venedig"', *Euphorion*, lii (1958–9), 378–96

H. Mayer: *Richard Wagner in Selbstzeugnissen und Bilddokumenten* (Hamburg, 1959; Eng. trans., 1972)

O. Daube: *Richard Wagner: 'Ich schreibe keine Symphonien mehr': Richard Wagners Lehrjahre nach den erhaltenen Dokumenten* (Cologne, 1960)

C. von Westernhagen: *Richard Wagners Dresdener Bibliothek 1842–1849: neue Dokumente zur Geschichte seines Schaffens* (Wiesbaden, 1966)

R. Hollinrake: 'The Title-Page of Wagner's "Mein Leben"', *ML*, li (1970), 415–22

M. Gregor-Dellin: *Wagner Chronik: Daten zu Leben und Werk* (Munich, 1972)

H. Conrad: 'Absturz aus Klingsors Zaubergarten: ein biographischer Beitrag zu den letzten Lebensjahren Richard Wagners', *Fränkischer Heimatbote* [monthly suppl. to *Nordbayerischer Kurier*], xi/8 (Bayreuth, 1978)

C. von Westernhagen: 'Wagner's Last Day', *MT*, cxx (1979), 395–7

G. Skelton: *Richard and Cosima Wagner: Biography of a Marriage* (London, 1982)

S. Spencer: 'Wagner in London (1)', *Wagner*, iii (1982), 98–123 [incl. previously unpubd material]

K.-H. Kröplin: *Richard Wagner 1813–1883: eine Chronik* (Leipzig, 1983, 2/1987)

M. Gregor-Dellin: 'Neue Wagner-Ermittlungen (Das Geheimnis der Mutter)', *Bayreuther Festspiele: Programmheft II. Parsifal* (Bayreuth, 1985), 21–32 [incl. Eng. trans.]

M. Eger: 'Richard Wagner und König Ludwig II.', *Richard-Wagner-Handbuch*, ed. U. Müller and P. Wapnewski (Stuttgart, 1986; Eng. trans., rev., 1992), 162–73

M. Kreckel: *Richard Wagner und die französischen Frühsozialisten* (Frankfurt, 1986)

U. Müller and P. Wapnewski, eds.: *Richard-Wagner-Handbuch* (Stuttgart, 1986; Eng. trans., rev., 1992 by J. Deathridge)

H. Erismann: *Richard Wagner in Zürich* (Zürich, 1987)

J. Thiery and U. Tröhler: 'Zweifel am Fortschrittsglauben. Der Tierversuchsgegner Richard Wagner: seine Zeitkritik und die Reaktion seiner Zeit', *Bayreuther Festspiele: Programmheft II. Parsifal* (Bayreuth, 1987), 1–64 [incl. Eng. trans.]

E. Kröplin: *Richard Wagner: theatralisches Leben und lebendiges Theater* (Leipzig, 1989)

E. Magee: *Richard Wagner and the Nibelungs* (Oxford, 1990)

B. Millington, ed.: *The Wagner Compendium* (London, 1992)

S. Williams: *Richard Wagner and Festival Theatre* (Westport, CT, 1994)

R. Bartlett: *Wagner and Russia* (Cambridge, 1995)

M.A. Weiner: *Richard Wagner and the Anti-Semitic Imagination* (Lincoln, NE, 1995, 2/1997)

J: Bayreuth: the Festspielhaus, its politics and influence

W. Schüler: *Der Bayreuther Kreis von seiner Entstehung bis zum Ausgang der wilhelminischen ära: Wagnerkult und Kulturreform im Geiste völkischer Weltanschauung* (Münster, 1971)

M. Karbaum: *Studien zur Geschichte der Bayreuther Festspiele* (Regensburg, 1976)

H. Mayer: *Richard Wagner in Bayreuth: 1876–1976* (Stuttgart, 1976; Eng. trans., 1976)

E. Voss: *Die Dirigenten der Bayreuther Festspiele* (Regensburg, 1976)

H. Zelinsky: *Richard Wagner – ein deutsches Thema* (Frankfurt, 1976, 3/1983)

J. Deathridge: 'Bayreuth's National Front', *Times Literary Supplement* (5 Aug 1977)

S. Grossmann-Vendrey: *Bayreuth in der deutschen Presse* (Regensburg, 1977–83)

R. Hartford: *Bayreuth: the Early Years* (London, 1980)

B.W. Wessling, ed.: *Bayreuth im Dritten Reich* (Weinheim and Basle, 1983)

H. Habel: *Festspielhaus und Wahnfried* (Munich, 1985)

F. Spotts: *Bayreuth: a History of the Wagner Festival* (New Haven, CT, 1994)

W. Wagner: *Lebens-Akte* (Munich, 1994; Eng. trans., 1994)

G. Wagner: *Wer nicht mit dem Wolf heult: Autobiographische Aufzeichnungen eines Wagner-Urenkels* (Cologne, 1997; Eng. trans., 1998)

N. Wagner: *Wagner-Theater* (Frankfurt, 1998; Eng. trans., 2000)

K: Production studies

A. Appia: *La mise en scène du drame wagnérien* (Paris, 1895); ed. E. Stadler, in *Schweizerische Gesellschaft für Theaterkultur*, xxviii–xxix (1962–3)

A. Appia: *Die Musik und die Inszenierung* (Munich, 1899; Fr. orig., Berne, 1963; Eng. trans., 1962)

F.A. Geissler: 'Wagner und die Opernregie', *Richard Wagner-Jb*, i (1906), 251–60

A. Heuss: 'Musik und Szene bei Wagner: ein Beispiel aus "Tristan und Isolde" und zugleich ein kleiner Beitrag zur Charakteristik Gustav Mahlers als Regisseur', *Die Musik*, xii/2 (1912–13), 207–13

E. Preetorius: *Richard Wagner: Bild und Vision* (Berlin, 1942)

K.H. Ruppel, ed.: *Wieland Wagner inszeniert Richard Wagner* (Konstanz, 1960)

K. Neupert: 'Die Besetzung der Bayreuther Festspiele 1876–1960', *Internationale Wagner Bibliographie: 1956–60*, ed. H. Barth (Bayreuth, 1961), 47–119

W. Wagner, ed.: *Richard Wagner und das neue Bayreuth* (Munich, 1962)

D. Steinbeck: *Inszenierungsformen des 'Tannhäuser' (1845–1904): Untersuchungen zur Systematik der Opernregie* (Regensburg, 1964)

G. Skelton: *Wagner at Bayreuth: Experiment and Tradition* (London, 1965, enlarged 2/1976/R)

D. Steinbeck, ed.: *Richard Wagners Tannhäuser-Szenarium: das Vorbild der Erstaufführungen mit der Kostümbeschreibung und den Dekorationsplänen* (Berlin, 1968)

P. Turing: *New Bayreuth* (London, 1969, 2/1971)

D. and M. Petzet: *Die Richard Wagner-Bühne König Ludwigs II.* (Munich, 1970)

W.E. Schäfer: *Wieland Wagner: Persönlichkeit und Leistung* (Tübingen, 1970)

D. Steinbeck: 'Richard Wagners "Lohengrin"-Szenarium', *Kleine Schriften der Gesellschaft für Theatergeschichte*, xxv (Berlin, 1972), 3–44

H. Barth, ed.: *Der Festspielhügel: 100 Jahre Bayreuther Festspiele in einer repräsentativen Dokumentation* (Bayreuth, 1973, 2/1976)

L. Lucas: *Die Festspiel-Idee Richard Wagners* (Regensburg, 1973)

G. Zeh: *Das Bayreuther Bühnenkostüm* (Munich, 1973)

D. Mack: *Der Bayreuther Inszenierungsstil* (Munich, 1976)

D. Mack, ed.: *Theaterarbeit an Wagners Ring* (Munich, 1978)

C.-F. Baumann: *Bühnentechnik im Bayreuther Festspielhaus* (Munich, 1980)

O.G. Bauer: *Richard Wagner: die Bühnenwerke von der Uraufführung bis heute* (Frankfurt, Berlin and Vienna, 1982; Eng. trans., 1983)

C. Osborne: *The World Theatre of Wagner* (Oxford, 1982)

M. Srocke: *Richard Wagner als Regisseur* (Berlin, 1988)

B. Millington and S. Spencer, eds.: *Wagner in Performance* (New Haven, CT, 1992)

L: Literary and philosophical studies

F. Nietzsche: *Der Fall Wagner* (Leipzig, 1888; Eng. trans., 1967)

J.L. Weston: *The Legends of the Wagner Drama: Studies in Mythology and Romance* (London, 1896)

W. Golther: *Richard Wagner als Dichter* (Berlin, 1904; Eng. trans., 1905)

R. Sternfeld: *Schiller und Wagner* (Berlin, 1905)

E. Dujardin: 'La revue wagnérienne', *ReM*, iv/11 (1922–3), 237–56; pubd separately (New York, 1977)

A. Drews: *Der Ideengehalt von Richard Wagners dramatischen Dichtungen im Zusammenhänge mitseinem Leben und seiner Weltanschauung, nebst einem Anhang: Nietzsche und Wagner* (Leipzig, 1931)

G. Woolley: *Richard Wagner et le symbolisme français* (Paris, 1931)

K. Jäckel: *Richard Wagner in der französischen Literatur* (Breslau, 1931–2)

G. Abraham: 'Nietzsche's Attitude to Wagner: a Fresh View', *ML*, xiii (1932), 64–74; repr. in *Slavonic and Romantic Music: Essays and Studies* (London, 1968), 313–22

P. Claudel: 'Richard Wagner: rêverie d'un poète français', *Revue de Paris* (15 July 1934); ed. M. Malicet (Paris, 1970)

H. Schneider: *Richard Wagner und das germanische Altertum* (Tübingen, 1939)

M. Gregor-Dellin: *Wagner und kein Ende: Richard Wagner im Spiegel von Thomas Manns Prosawerk: eine Studie* (Bayreuth, 1958)

E. Bloch: 'Paradoxa und Pastorale in Wagners Musik', *Merkur*, xiii (1959),405–35; repr. in *Verfremdungen*, i (Frankfurt, 1962), and *Literarische Aufsätze* (Frankfurt, 1965); Eng. trans., 1985

E. Mann, ed.: T. Mann *Wagner und unsere Zeit: Aufsätze, Betrachtungen, Briefe* (Frankfurt, 1963/*R*); Eng. trans., enlarged, as *Thomas Mann: Pro and Contra Wagner* (London, 1985)

L. Siegel: 'Wagner and the Romanticism of E.T.A. Hoffmann', *MQ*, li (1965), 597–613

M. Gregor-Dellin: *Richard Wagner: die Revolution als Oper* (Munich, 1973)

K.G. Just: 'Richard Wagner – ein Dichter? Marginalien zum Opernlibretto des 19. Jahrhunderts', *Richard Wagner: von der Oper zum Musikdrama*, ed. S. Kunze (Berne and Munich, 1978), 79–94

H. Mayer: *Richard Wagner: Mitwelt und Nachwelt* (Stuttgart, 1978)

H. Zelinsky: 'Die "feuerkur" des Richard Wagner oder die "neue religion" der "Erlösung" durch "Vernichtung"', *Richard Wagner: wie antisemitisch darf ein Künstler sein?*, ed. H.-K. Metzger and R. Riehn (Munich, 1978), 79–112

A.D. Sessa: *Richard Wagner and the English* (Rutherford, NJ, 1979)

M. Tanner: 'The Total Work of Art', *The Wagner Companion*, ed. P. Burbidge and R. Sutton (London, 1979), 140–224

H. Barth, ed.: *Bayreuther Dramaturgie: Der Ring des Nibelungen* (Stuttgart, 1980)

D. Cormack: 'Thomas Mann, Hanns Eisler and the "New Bayreuth"', *Wagner*, ii (1981), 44–63

D. Borchmeyer: *Das Theater Richard Wagners: Idee – Dichtung – Wirkung* (Stuttgart, 1982; Eng. trans., 1991)

R. Furness: *Wagner and Literature* (Manchester, 1982)

R. Hollinrake: *Nietzsche, Wagner and the Philosophy of Pessimism* (London, 1982)

D. Ingenschay-Goch: *Richard Wagners neu erfundener Mythos: zur Rezeption und Reproduktion des germanischen Mythos in seinen Operntexten* (Bonn, 1982)

H. Lloyd-Jones: 'Wagner', *Blood for the Ghosts* (London, 1982), 126–42 [Greek influences on Wagner]

R. Franke: *Richard Wagners Zürcher Kunstschriften* (Hamburg, 1983)

S. Kunze: *Der Kunstbegriff Richard Wagners* (Regensburg, 1983)

B. Magee: *The Philosophy of Schopenhauer* (Oxford, 1983, 2/1997) [incl. substantial appx on Schopenhauer and Wagner]

A.D. Aberbach: *The Ideas of Richard Wagner* (Lanham, MD, 1984, 2/1988)

I. Gillespie: 'The Theory and Practice of "Wahn"', *Wagner*, v (1984), 79–95

M. Vogel: *Nietzsche und Wagner: ein deutsches Lesebuch* (Bonn, 1984)

J. Katz: *Richard Wagner: Vorbote des Antisemitismus* (Königstein, 1985; Eng.trans., 1986, as *The Darker Side of Genius*)

C. Suneson: *Richard Wagner och den indiska tankevärlden* (Stockholm, 1985; Ger. trans., 1989)

A. Ingenhoff: *Drama oder Epos? Richard Wagners Gattungstheorie des musikalischen Dramas* (Tübingen, 1987)

U. Bermbach: 'Die Destruktion der Institutionen: überlegungen zum politischen Gehalt von Richard Wagners "Ring des Nibelungen"', *Bayreuther Festspiele: Programmheft III. Die Walküre* (Bayreuth, 1988), 13–66 [incl. Eng. trans.]

M. Eger: '*Wenn ich Wagnern den Krieg mache ...*': der Fall Nietzsche und das Menschliche, Allzumenschliche (Vienna, 1988), 129–67

U. Bermbach, ed.: *In den Trümmern der eigenen Welt: Richard Wagners 'Der Ring des Nibelungen'* (Berlin, 1989)

U. Müller and U. Müller, eds.: *Richard Wagner und sein Mittelalter* (Salzburg, 1989)

U. Bermbach: 'Wagner und Lukács: über die Ästhetisierung von Politik und die Politisierung von Ästhetik', *Bayreuther Festspiele: Programmheft II. Lohengrin* (Bayreuth, 1990), 1–27 [incl. Eng. trans.]

S. Corse: *Wagner and the New Consciousness: Language and Love in the 'Ring'* (Rutherford, NJ, Madison, WI, and Teaneck, NJ, 1990)

E. Lippman: 'Wagner's Conception of the Dream', *JM*, viii (1990), 54–81

J.-J. Nattiez: *Wagner androgyne* (Paris, 1990; Eng. trans., 1993)

L.J. Rather: *Reading Wagner: a Study in the History of Ideas* (Baton Rouge, LA, 1990)

P.L. Rose: *Revolutionary Antisemitism in Germany from Kant to Wagner* (Princeton, NJ, 1990)

P.L. Rose: *Wagner: Race and Revolution* (London, 1992)

A.D. Aberbach: *Richard Wagner's Religious Ideas: a Spiritual Journey* (Lewiston, NY, and Lampeter, 1996)

D.J. Levin: *Richard Wagner, Fritz Lang, and the Nibelungen: the Dramaturgy of Disavowal* (Princeton, NJ, 1998)

M: Analysis and criticism: general studies

W.A. Ellis: *Richard Wagner as Poet, Musician and Mystic* (London, 1887)

H. von Wolzogen: *Wagneriana: gesammelte Aufsätze über Richard Wagners Werke vom Ring bis zum Gral* (Leipzig, 1888/R)

L. Torchi: *Riccardo Wagner: studio critico* (Bologna, 1890, 2/1913)

H.E. Krehbiel: *Studies in the Wagnerian Drama* (New York, 1891/R, 2/1893)

H.S. Chamberlain: *Das Drama Richard Wagners: eine Anregung* (Leipzig, 1892, 3/1908/R; Eng. trans., 1915)

A. Prüfer: *Die Bühnenfestspiele in Bayreuth* (Leipzig, 1899, enlarged, 1909, as *Das Werk von Bayreuth*)

W.J. Henderson: *Richard Wagner: his Life and his Dramas* (New York, 1901, 2/1923/R)

A. Seidl: *Wagneriana* (Berlin, 1901–2)

G. Adler: *Richard Wagner: Vorlesungen gehalten an der Universität zu Wien* (Munich, 1904, 2/1923)

H. von Wolzogen: *Musikalisch-dramatische Parallelen: Beiträge zur Erkenntnis von der Musik als Ausdruck* (Leipzig, 1906)

A. Seidl: *Neue Wagneriana: gesammelte Aufsätze und Studien* (Regensburg, 1914)

P. Bekker: *Richard Wagner: das Leben im Werke* (Stuttgart, 1924; Eng. trans., 1931)

A. Lorenz: *Das Geheimnis der Form bei Richard Wagner*, i: *Der musikalische Aufbau des Bühnenfestspieles Der Ring des Nibelungen* (Berlin, 1924); ii: *Der musikalische Aufbau von Richard Wagners 'Tristan und Isolde'* (Berlin, 1926); iii: *Der musikalische Aufbau von Richard Wagners 'Die Meistersinger von Nürnberg'* (Berlin, 1930); iv: *Der musikalische Aufbau von Richard Wagners 'Parsifal'* (Berlin, 1933)

O. Strobel: *Richard Wagner über sein Schaffen: ein Beitrag zur 'Künstlerästhetik'* (Munich, 1924)

O. Strobel: 'Richard Wagners Originalpartituren', *AMz*, lv (1928), 307–11

H. Pfitzner: *Werk und Wiedergabe*, Gesammelte Schriften, iii (Augsburg, 1929, 2/1969)

V. d'Indy: *Richard Wagner et son influence sur l'art musical français* (Paris, 1930)

W. Engelsmann: *Wagners klingendes Universum* (Potsdam, 1933)

L. Gilman: *Wagner's Operas* (New York, 1937)

E. Newman: *Wagner Nights* (London, 1949/R); as *The Wagner Operas* (New York, 1949/R)

O. Strobel: 'Eingebung und bewusste Arbeit im musikalischen Schaffen Richard Wagners', *Bayreuther Festspielbuch 1951*, 88–95

P.A. Loos: *Richard Wagner: Vollendung und Tragik der deutschen Romantik* (Berne, 1952)

J.M. Stein: *Richard Wagner & the Synthesis of the Arts* (Detroit, 1960/R)

C. von Westernhagen: *Vom Holländer zum Parsifal: neue Wagner-Studien* (Freiburg, 1962)

H. Gál: *Richard Wagner: Versuch einer Würdigung* (Frankfurt, 1963; Eng. trans., 1976)

C. Dahlhaus: 'Wagners Begriff der "dichterisch-musikalischen Periode"', *Beiträge zur Geschichte der Musikanschauung im 19. Jahrhundert*, ed. W. Salmen, i (Regensburg, 1965), 179–87

H. Mayer: *Anmerkungen zu Wagner* (Frankfurt, 1966)

H.F. Redlich: 'Wagnerian Elements in pre-Wagnerian Operas', *Essays Presented to Egon Wellesz*, ed. J. Westrup (Oxford, 1966), 145–56

C. Dahlhaus: 'Eduard Hanslick und der musikalische Formbegriff', *Mf*, xx (1967), 145–53

K. Overhoff: *Die Musikdramen Richard Wagners: eine thematischmusikalische Interpretation* (Salzburg, 1967, 2/1984)

M. Geck: 'Richard Wagner und die ältere Musik', *Die Ausbreitung des Historismus über die Musik*, ed. W. Wiora (Regensburg, 1969), 123–40

R. Raphael: *Richard Wagner* (New York, 1969)

Verdi–Wagner: Rome 1969 [AnMc, no.11 (1972)]

C. Dahlhaus: *Die Bedeutung des Gestischen in Wagners Musikdramen* (Munich, 1970)

C. Dahlhaus: 'Soziologische Dechiffrierung von Musik: zu Theodor W. Adornos Wagnerkritik', *IRMAS*, i (1970), 137–47

C. Dahlhaus: 'Wagner and Program Music', *Studies in Romanticism*, ix (1970), 3–20; Ger. orig., in *JbSIM 1973*, 50–63

C. Dahlhaus, ed.: *Das Drama Richard Wagners als musikalisches Kunstwerk* (Regensburg, 1970)

S. Kunze: 'Naturszenen in Wagners Musikdrama', *GfMKB: Bonn 1970*, 199–207

E. Voss: *Studien zur Instrumentation Richard Wagners* (Regensburg, 1970)

C. Dahlhaus: *Richard Wagners Musikdramen* (Velber, nr Hanover, 1971, 2/1985; Eng. trans., 1979)

C. Dahlhaus: *Wagners Konzeption des musikalischen Dramas* (Regensburg, 1971)

A. Sommer: *Die Komplikationen des musikalischen Rhythmus in den Bühnenwerken Richard Wagners* (Giebing, 1971)

R. Bailey: 'The Evolution of Wagner's Compositional Procedure after Lohengrin', *IMSCR XI: Copenhagen 1972*, 240–46

U. Jung: *Die Rezeption der Kunst Richard Wagners in Italien* (Regensburg, 1974)

J. Deathridge: 'The Nomenclature of Wagner's Sketches', *PRMA*, ci (1974–5), 75–83

K. Kropfinger: *Wagner und Beethoven: Untersuchungen zur Beethoven-Rezeption Richard Wagners* (Regensburg, 1975; Eng. trans., rev., 1991)

S. Spencer, ed.: *Wagner 1976: a Celebration of the Bayreuth Festival* (London, 1976)

H.F. Garten: *Wagner the Dramatist* (London, 1977)

P. Boulez: 'Anmerkung zur musikalischen Struktur', *Theaterarbeit an Wagners Ring*, ed. D. Mack (Munich, 1978), 243

S. Kunze: 'Über den Kunstcharakter des Wagnerschen Musikdramas', *Richard Wagner: von der Oper zum Musikdrama* (Berne and Munich, 1978), 9–24

H.-K. Metzger and R. Riehn, eds.: *Richard Wagner: wie antisemitisch darf ein Künstler sein?* (Munich, 1978)

D.R. Murray: 'Major Analytical Approaches to Wagner's Musical Style: a Critique', *MR*, xxxix (1978), 211–22

E. Voss: 'Nocheinmal: das Geheimnis der Form bei Richard Wagner', *Theaterarbeit an Wagners Ring*, ed. D. Mack (Munich, 1978), 251–67; Eng. trans., *Wagner*, iv (1983), 66–79

P. Wapnewski: *Der traurige Gott: Richard Wagner in seinen Helden* (Munich, 1978)

P. Burbidge and R. Sutton, eds.: *The Wagner Companion* (London, 1979)

R. Holloway: *Debussy and Wagner* (London, 1979)

N. Josephson: 'Tonale Strukturen im musikdramatischen Schaffen Richard Wagners', *Mf*, xxxii (1979), 141–9

R.T. Laudon: *Sources of the Wagnerian Synthesis: a Study of the Franco-German Tradition in 19th-Century Opera* (Munich and Salzburg, 1979)

A. Newcomb: 'The Birth of Music out of the Spirit of Drama: an Essay in Wagnerian Formal Analysis', *19CM*, v (1981–2), 38–66

D. Borchmeyer: *Das Theater Richard Wagners* (Munich, 1982; Eng. trans., 1991)

R. Brinkmann: '"einen Schluss machen!" Über externe Schlüsse bei Wagner', *Festschrift Heinz Becker*, ed. J. Schläder and R. Quandt (Laaber, 1982), 179–90

R. Brinkmann: 'Richard Wagner der Erzähler', *ÖMz*, xxxvii (1982), 297–306

M. Ewans: *Wagner and Aeschylus: the 'Ring' and the 'Oresteia'* (London, 1982)

C. Dahlhaus: 'Wagner's "A Communication to my Friends": Reminiscence and Adaptation', *MT*, cxxiv (1983), 89–92

C. Dahlhaus and E. Voss, eds.: *Wagnerliteratur – Wagner-Forschung: Munich 1983*

J. Deathridge: 'Cataloguing Wagner', *MT*, cxxiv (1983), 92–6

F.W. Glass: *The Fertilizing Seed: Wagner's Concept of the Poetic Intent* (Ann Arbor, 1983)

A. Newcomb: 'Those Images that Yet Fresh Images Beget', *JM*, ii (1983), 227–45

A. Whittall: 'Wagner's Great Transition? From *Lohengrin* to *Das Rheingold'*, *MAn*, ii (1983), 269–80

P. Dennison, ed.: *The Richard Wagner Centenary in Australia* (Adelaide, 1985)

M.C. Tusa: 'Richard Wagner and Weber's Euryanthe', *19CM*, ix (1985–6), 206–21

L.R. Shaw, N.R. Cirillo and M.S. Miller, eds.: *Wagner in Retrospect: a Centennial Reappraisal* (Amsterdam, 1987)

J. Warrack: 'The Influence of French Grand Opera on Wagner', *Music in Paris in the Eighteen-Thirties*, ed. P. Bloom (Stuyvesant, NY, 1987), 575–87

C. Abbate: 'Erik's Dream and Tannhäuser's Journey', *Reading Opera*, ed. A. Groos and R. Parker (Princeton, NJ, 1988), 129–67

T.S. Grey: 'Wagner, the Overture, and the Aesthetics of Musical Form', *19CM*, xii (1988–9), 3–22

C. Abbate: 'Opera as Symphony, a Wagnerian Myth', *Analyzing Opera: Verdi and Wagner*, ed. C. Abbate and R. Parker (Berkeley, 1989), 92–124

C. Abbate: 'Wagner, "On Modulation", and *Tristan'*, *COJ*, i (1989), 33–58

A. Newcomb: 'Ritornello Ritornato: a Variety of Wagnerian Refrain Form', *Analyzing Opera: Verdi and Wagner*, ed. C. Abbate and R. Parker (Berkeley, 1989), 202–21

C. Osborne: *The Complete Operas of Richard Wagner* (London, 1990)

A. Whittall: 'Wagner's Later Stage Works', *NOHM*, ix (1990), 257–321

H.M. Brown: *Leitmotiv and Drama: Wagner, Brecht, and the Limits of 'Epic' Theatre* (Oxford, 1991)

K. Ellis: *Music Criticism in Nineteenth-Century France* (Cambridge, 1995)

T.S. Grey: *Wagner's Musical Prose: Texts and Contexts* (Cambridge, 1995)

S. McClatchie: *Analyzing Wagner's Operas: Alfred Lorenz and German Nationalist Ideology* (Rochester, NY, 1994)

N: Analysis and criticism: individual studies

Early operas: Die Hochzeit to Lohengrin

W. Golther: 'Rienzi: ein musikalisches Drama', *Die Musik*, i (1901–2),1833–9

F. Muncker: 'Richard Wagners Operntext "Die Hochzeit"', *Die Musik*, i (1901–2), 1824–9

W. Altmann: 'Richard Wagner und die Berliner General Intendantur: Verhandlungen über den "Fliegender Holländer" und "Tannhäuser"', *Die Musik*, ii/2 (1902–3), 331–45; ii/3 (1902–3), 92–109, 304–17

W. Golther: 'Die französische und die deutsche Tannhäuser-Dichtung', *Die Musik*, ii/3 (1902–3), 271–82

H. Dinger: 'Zu Richard Wagners "Rienzi"', *Richard Wagner-Jb*, iii (1908), 88–132

E. Istel: 'Richard Wagners Oper "Das Liebesverbot" auf Grund der handschriftlichen Originalpartitur dargestellt', *Die Musik*, viii/4 (1908–9), 3–47

H. Porges: 'Über Richard Wagner's "Lohengrin"', *Bayreuther Blätter*, xxxii (1909), 173–201

E. Istel: 'Wagners erste Oper "Die Hochzeit" auf Grund der autographen Partitur dargestellt', *Die Musik*, ix/2 (1909–10), 331–51

W. Krienitz: *Richard Wagners 'Feen'* (Munich, 1910)

E. Istel: 'Autographe Regiebemerkungen Wagners zum "Fliegenden Holländer" zum ersten male veröffentlicht', *Die Musik*, xii/2 (1912–13), 214–19

J.G. Robertson: 'The Genesis of Wagner's Drama "Tannhäuser"', *Modern Language Review*, xviii (1923), 458–70

O. Strobel: 'Wagners Prosaentwurf zum "Fliegenden Holländer"', *Bayreuther Blätter*, lvi (1933), 157–60; Eng.trans., *Wagner*, ii (1981), 26–9

A. Lorenz: 'Der musikalische Aufbau von Wagners "Lohengrin"', *Bayreuther Festspielführer 1936*, 189–98; Eng. trans., *Wagner*, ii (1981), 40–43

O. Strobel: 'Die Urgestalt des "Lohengrin": Wagners erster dichterischer Entwurf', *Bayreuther Festspielführer 1936*, 141–71; Eng. trans., *Wagner*, iv (1983), 34–49

G. Abraham: '"The Flying Dutchman": Original Version', *ML*, xx (1939), 412–19

G. Graarud: '"Sandwike ist's, genau kenn' ich die Bucht!"', *Bayreuther Festspielführer 1939*, 61–72

H. Engel: 'Über Richard Wagners Oper "Das Liebesverbot"', *Festschrift Friedrich Blume*, ed. A.A. Abert and W. Pfannkuch (Kassel, 1963), 80–91

G. Abraham: 'Wagner's Second Thoughts', *Slavonic and Romantic Music: Essays and Studies* (London, 1968), 294–312 [on rev. of *Der fliegende Holländer* and *Tannhäuser*]

G. Abraham: 'A Lost Wagner Aria', *MT*, cx (1969), 927–9

M. Geck: 'Rienzi-Philologie', *Das Drama Richard Wagners als musikalisches Kunstwerk*, ed. C. Dahlhaus (Regensburg, 1970), 183–96

C. Hopkinson: *Tannhäuser: an Examination of 36 Editions* (Tutzing, 1973)

P.S. Machlin: 'Wagner, Durand and "The Flying Dutchman": the 1852 Revisions of the Overture', *ML*, lv (1974), 410–28

P.S. Machlin: *Genesis, Revisions, and Publication History of Wagner's 'The Flying Dutchman'* (diss., U. of California, Berkeley, 1975)

S. Spencer: 'Tannhäuser: mediävistische Handlung in drei Aufzügen', *Wagner 1976: a Celebration of the Bayreuth Festival* (London, 1976), 40–53

R. Strohm, ed.: *Dokumente und Texte zu 'Rienzi, der Letzte der Tribunen'*, Richard Wagner: Sämtliche Werke, xxiii (Mainz, 1976)

J. Deathridge: *Wagner's Rienzi: a Reappraisal Based on a Study of the Sketches and Drafts* (Oxford, 1977)

R. Strohm: 'Dramatic Time and Operatic Form in Wagner's "Tannhäuser"', *PRMA*, civ (1977–8), 1–10

J. Deathridge: 'Fragmente über Fragmentarisches: zur "Lohengrin"-Kompositionsskizze', *Bayerische Staatsoper: Lohengrin – Programmheft zur Neuinszenierung* (Munich, 1978), 41

J. Deathridge: 'Eine verschollene Wagner-Arie?', *Melos/NZM*, iv (1978), 208–14

L. Finscher: 'Wagner der Opernkomponist: von den "Feen" zum "Rienzi"', *Richard Wagner: von der Oper zum Musikdrama*, ed. S. Kunze (Berne and Munich, 1978), 25–46

R. Strohm: 'Zur Werkgeschichte des "Tannhäuser"', *Bayreuther Festspiele: Programmheft III. Tannhäuser* (Bayreuth, 1978), 12–13, 64–76 [incl. Eng. trans.]

I. Vetter: 'Holländer-Metamorphosen', *Melos/NZM*, iv (1978), 206–8

I. Vetter: 'Der "Ahasverus des Ozeans" – musikalisch unerlöst? Der fliegende Holländer und sein Revisionen', *Bayreuther Festspiele: Programmheft II. Der fliegende Holländer* (Bayreuth, 1979), 70–79 [incl. Eng. trans.]

L'avant-scène opéra, no.30 (1980) [*Der fliegende Holländer* issue]

W. Breig: 'Das "verdichtete Bild des ganzen Dramas": die Ursprünge von Wagners "Holländer"-Musik und die Senta-Ballade', *Festschrift Heinz Becker*, ed. J. Schläder and R. Quandt (Laaber, 1982), 162–78

A. Csampai and D. Holland, eds.: *Rororo Opernbücher: Der fliegende Holländer* (Reinbek bei Hamburg, 1982)

N. John, ed.: *The Flying Dutchman* (London, 1982) [ENO opera guide]

I. Vetter: *Der fliegende Holländer von Richard Wagner: Entstehung, Bearbeitung, Überlieferung* (diss., Technische Universität, Berlin, 1982)

C. Abbate: 'The Parisian "Venus" and the "Paris" Tannhäuser', *JAMS*, xxxvi (1983), 73–123

B. Millington: 'Did Wagner Really Sell his "Dutchman" Story? A Re-examination of the Paris Transaction', *Wagner*, iv (1983), 114–27

S. Spencer: '"Die hohe Braut": an Unpublished Sketch', *Wagner*, iv (1983), 13–26

C. Abbate: *The 'Parisian' Tannhäuser* (diss., Princeton U., 1984)

L'avant-scène opéra, nos. 63–4 (1984) [*Tannhäuser* issue]

R. Brinkmann: 'Sentas Traumerzählung', *Bayreuther Festspiele: Programmheft I. Der fliegende Holländer* (Bayreuth, 1984), 1–17 [incl. Eng. trans.]

'Richard Wagner: Der Venusberg', *Bayreuther Festspiele: Programmheft I. Tannhäuser* (Bayreuth, 1985), 1–14 [transcr. of previously unpubd prose draft of *Tannhäuser*] [incl. Eng. trans.]

B. Millington: '"The Flying Dutchman", "Le vaisseau fantôme" and other Nautical Yarns', *MT*, cxxvii (1986), 131–5

P. Bloom: 'The Fortunes of the Flying Dutchman in France', *Wagner*, viii (1987), 42–66

N. John, ed.: *Tannhäuser* (London, 1988) [ENO opera guide]

J. Deathridge: 'Through the Looking Glass: Some Remarks on the First Complete Draft of *Lohengrin*', *Analyzing Opera*, ed. C. Abbate and R. Parker (Berkeley, 1989), 56–91

B. Millington: 'An Introduction to the Paris "Tannhäuser"', *Tannhäuser*, DG 427 625–2 (1989), 25–33 [disc notes]

J. Fischer, ed.: *Richard Wagners unvollendete Jugendoper 'Männerlist grösser als Frauenlist oder Die glücklicher Bärenfamilie'* (Berlin, 1996) [detailing the rediscovery of sketches]

Der Ring des Nibelungen

H. von Wolzogen: *Thematischer Leitfaden durch die Musik von R. Wagners Festspiel 'Der Ring des Nibelungen'* (Leipzig, 1876; Eng. trans., 1882)

G.B. Shaw: *The Perfect Wagnerite: a Commentary on the Ring of the Nibelungs* (London, 1898, 4/1923/R)

C. Saint-Saëns: 'Bayreuth und der Ring des Nibelungen', *Die Musik*, i (1901–2), 751–63, 879–84

W. Golther: *Die sagengeschichtlichen Grundlagen der Ringdichtung Richard Wagners* (Berlin, 1902)

W.A. Ellis: 'Die verschiedenen Fassungen von "Siegfrieds Tod"', *Die Musik*, iii/2 (1903–4), 239–51, 315–31

O. Strobel: 'Die Originalpartitur von Richard Wagners "Rheingold"', *Bayreuther Festspielführer 1928*, 47–55

O. Strobel: 'Die Kompositionsskizzen zum "Ring des Nibelungen"; ein Blick in die Musikerwerkstatt Richard Wagners', *Bayreuther Festspielführer 1930*, 114–22

O. Strobel, ed.: *Richard Wagner: Skizzen und Entwürfe zur Ring-Dichtung, mit der Dichtung 'Der Junge Siegfried'* (Munich, 1930) [see also O. Strobel, *Die Musik*, xxv (1932–3), 336–41]

O. Strobel: '"Winterstürme wichen dem Wonnemond": zur Genesis von Siegmunds Lenzgesang', *Bayreuther Blätter*, liii (1930), 123–7

O. Strobel: 'Aus Wagners Musikerwerkstatt: Betrachtungen über die Kompositionsskizzen zum "Ring des Nibelungen"', *AMz*, lviii (1931), 463–5, 479–82, 495–8

O. Strobel: 'Vom Werden der "Ring"-Dichtung: Authentisches zur Entstehungsgeschichte des Bühnenfestspiels', *Bayreuther Festspielführer 1931*, 77–90

A. Buesst: *Richard Wagner: the Nibelung's Ring* (London, 1932, 2/1952)

O. Strobel: 'Zur Entstehungsgeschichte der Götterdämmerung: unbekannte Dokumente aus Wagners Dichterwerkstatt', *Die Musik*, xxv (1932–3), 336–41

W. Serauky: 'Die Todesverkündigungsszene in Richard Wagners "Walküre" als musikalisch-geistige Achse des Werkes', *Mf*, xii (1959), 143–51

R. Donington: *Wagner's 'Ring' and its Symbols: the Music and the Myth* (London, 1963, enlarged 3/1974/R)

C. von Westernhagen: 'Die Kompositions-Skizze zu "Siegfrieds Tod" aus dem Jahre 1850', *NZM*, Jg.124 (1963), 178–82

R. Bailey: 'Wagner's Musical Sketches for "Siegfrieds Tod"', *Studies in Music History: Essays for Oliver Strunk*, ed. H. Powers (Princeton, NJ, 1968), 459–94

C. Dahlhaus: 'Formprinzipien in Wagners "Ring des Nibelungen"', *Beiträge zur Geschichte der Oper*, ed. H. Becker (Regensburg, 1969), 95–129

T. Kneif: 'Zur Deutung der Rheintöchter in Wagners *Ring*', *AMw*, xxvi (1969), 297–306; Eng. trans., *Wagner*, x (1989), 21–8

D. Coren: *A Study of Richard Wagner's 'Siegfried'* (diss., U. of California, Berkeley, 1971)

R. Brinkmann: '"Drei der Fragen stell'ich mir frei": zur Wanderer-Szene im 1. Akt von Wagners "Siegfried"', *JbSIM 1973*, 120–62

W. Breig: *Studien zur Entstehungsgeschichte von Wagners 'Ring des Nibelungen'* (diss., U. of Freiburg, 1973)

C. von Westernhagen: *Die Entstehung des 'Ring', dargestellt an den Kompositionsskizzen Richard Wagners* (Zürich, 1973; Eng. trans., 1976)

P. Nitsche: 'Klangefarbe und Form: das Walhallthema in Rheingold und Walküre', *Melos/NZM*, i (1975), 83–8

L'avant-scène opéra, nos. 6–7 (1976) [*Das Rheingold* issue]

W. Breig and H. Fladt, eds.: *Dokumente zur Entstehungsgeschichte des Bühnenfestspiels Der Ring des Nibelungen*, Richard Wagner: Sämtliche Werke, xxix/1 (Mainz, 1976)

J. Culshaw: *Reflections on Wagner's Ring* (London, 1976)

L'avant-scène opéra, no.8 (1977) [*Die Walküre* issue]; no.12 (1977) [*Siegfried* issue]

J. Deathridge: 'Wagner's Sketches for the "Ring"', *MT*, cxviii (1977), 383–9

J.M. Knapp: 'The Instrumentation Draft of Wagner's "Das Rheingold"', *JAMS*, xxx (1977), 272–95

R. Bailey: 'The Structure of the "Ring" and its Evolution', *19CM*, i (1977–8), 48–61

L'avant-scène opéra, nos.13–14 (1978) [*Götterdämmerung* issue]

R. Brinkmann: 'Mythos – Geschichte – Natur: Zeitkonstellationen im "Ring"', *Richard Wagner: von der Oper zum Musikdrama*, ed. S. Kunze (Berne and Munich, 1978), 61–77

J.L. DiGaetani, ed.: *Penetrating Wagner's Ring: an Anthology* (Rutherford, NJ, Madison, WI, and Teaneck, NJ, 1978)

D. Cooke: *I Saw the World End* (London, 1979)

W. Breig: 'Der "Rheintöchtergesang" in Wagners "Rheingold"', *AMw*, xxxvii (1980), 241–63

D. Coren: 'Inspiration and Calculation in the Genesis of Wagner's "Siegfried"', *Studies in Musicology in Honor of Otto E. Albrecht*, ed. J.W. Hill (Kassel, 1980), 266–87

W. Kinderman: 'Dramatic Recapitulation in Wagner's "Götterdämmerung"', *19CM*, iv (1980–81), 101–12

L.J. Rather: *The Dream of Self-Destruction: Wagner's 'Ring' and the Modern World* (Baton Rouge, LA, 1981)

S. Spencer: '"Zieh hin! Ich kann dich nicht halten!"', *Wagner*, ii (1981), 98–120

P. McCreless: *Wagner's Siegfried: its Drama, History, and Music* (Ann Arbor, 1982)

W.-D. Schäfer: 'Syntaktische und semantische Bedingungen der Motivinstrumentation in Wagners *Ring*', *Festschrift Heinz Becker*, ed. J. Schläder and R. Quandt (Laaber, 1982), 191–204

D. Coren: 'The Texts of Wagner's "Der junge Siegfried" and "Siegfried"', *19CM*, vi (1982–3), 17–30

C. Dahlhaus: 'Tonalität und Form in Wagner's "Ring des Nibelungen"', *AMw*, xl (1983), 165–73

N. John, ed.: *Die Walküre* (London, 1983) [ENO opera guide]

J.-J. Nattiez: *Tétralogies – Wagner, Boulez, Chéreau: essai sur l'infidélité* (Paris, 1983)

N. John, ed.: *Siegfried* (London, 1984) [ENO opera guide]

S. Kester: *An Examination of the Themes of Love, Power and Salvation in Richard Wagner's 'The Ring of the Nibelung': a Study of a Failed Individuation Process* (diss., U. of Western Australia, 1984)

N. John, ed.: *The Rhinegold* (London, 1985) [ENO opera guide]

N. John, ed.: *Twilight of the Gods* (London, 1985) [ENO opera guide]

H.R. Vaget: 'Erlösung durch Liebe: Wagners "Ring" und Goethes "Faust"', *Bayreuther Festspiele: Programmheft VI. Götterdämmerung* (Bayreuth, 1985), 14–31 [incl. Eng. trans.]

W. Darcy: 'The Pessimism of the *Ring*', *OQ*, iv/2 (1986), 24–48

D. Borchmeyer, ed.: *Wege des Mythos in der Moderne: Richard Wagner 'Der Ring des Nibelungen'* (Munich, 1987)

W. Darcy: '"Alles was ist, endet!" Erda's Prophecy of World Destruction', *Bayreuther Festspiele: Programmheft II. Das Rheingold* (Bayreuth, 1988), 67–92

D.A. White: *The Turning Wheel: a Study of Contracts and Oaths in Wagner's 'Ring'* (Selinsgrove, PA, 1988)

C. Wintle: 'The Numinous in *Götterdämmerung*', *Reading Opera*, ed. A. Groos and R. Parker (Princeton, NJ, 1988)

H. Richardson, ed.: *New Studies in Richard Wagner's 'The Ring of the Nibelung'* (Lewiston, NY, 1991)

W. Darcy: *Wagner's 'Das Rheingold'* (Oxford, 1993)

S. Spencer and B. Millington, eds.: *Wagner's 'Ring of the Nibelung': a Companion* (London, 1993)

Tristan und Isolde

H. von Wolzogen: *Richard Wagner's Tristan und Isolde: ein Leitfaden durch Sage, Dichtung und Musik* (Leipzig, 1880; Eng. trans., 1884)

H. Porges: 'Tristan und Isolde', *Bayreuther Blätter*, xxv (1902), 186–211; xxvi (1903), 23–48, 241–70; ed. H. von Wolzogen (Leipzig, 1906)

W. Golther: 'Zur Entstehung von Richard Wagners Tristan', *Die Musik*, v/4 (1905–6), 3–16

L. Lehmann: *Studie zu 'Tristan und Isolde'* (Wittenberg, c1906)

A. Prüfer: 'Novalis Hymnen an die Nacht in ihren Beziehungen zu Wagners Tristan und Isolde', *Richard Wagner-Jb*, i (1906), 290–304

W. Golther: *Tristan und Isolde in den Dichtungen des Mittelalters und der neuen Zeit* (Leipzig, 1907)

E. Kurth: *Romantische Harmonik und ihre Krise in Wagners 'Tristan'* (Berlin, 1920, 2/1923/R)

H.F. Peyser: '"Tristan", First-Hand', *MQ*, xi (1925), 418–26

J. Kerman: 'Opera as Symphonic Poem', *Opera as Drama* (New York, 1956/R, 2/1988), chap. 7

V. Levi: *Tristano e Isotta di Riccardo Wagner* (Venice, 1958)

M. Vogel: *Der Tristan-Akkord und die Krise der modernen Harmonie-Lehre* (Düsseldorf, 1962)

H. Scharschuch: *Gesamtanalyse der Harmonik von Richard Wagners Musikdrama 'Tristan und Isolde': unter spezifischer Berücksichtigung der Sequenztechnik des Tristanstiles* (Regensburg, 1963)

H. Truscott: 'Wagner's "Tristan" and the Twentieth Century', *MR*, xxiv (1963), 75–85

E. Zuckerman: *The First Hundred Years of Wagner's Tristan* (New York, 1964)

W. Wagner, ed.: *Hundert Jahre Tristan: Neunzehn Essays* (Emsdetten, 1965)

W.J. Mitchell: 'The Tristan Prelude: Techniques and Structure', *Music Forum*, i (1967), 162–203

R. Bailey: *The Genesis of Tristan und Isolde, and a Study of Wagner's Sketches and Drafts for the First Act* (diss., Princeton U., 1969)

E. Voss: 'Wagner's Striche im Tristan', *NZM*, Jg.132 (1971), 644–7

R. Jackson: 'Leitmotive and Form in the "Tristan" Prelude', *MR*, xxxvi (1975), 42–53

C. Dahlhaus: '"Tristan"-Harmonik und Tonalität', *Melos/NZM*, iv (1978), 215–19

J. Deathridge: '"Im übrigen darf ich wohl hoffen, dass Sie mich nicht eben gerade für einen Honorararbeiter halten …": Zur Entstehung der "Tristan"-Partitur', *Bayerische Staatsoper: Tristan Programmheft zur Neuinszenierung* (Munich, 1980), 42

L'avant-scène opéra, nos. 34–5 (1981) [*Tristan und Isolde* issue]

N. John, ed.: *Tristan and Isolde* (London, 1981) [ENO opera guide]

P. Wapnewski: *Tristan der Held Richard Wagners* (Berlin, 1981)

C. Abbate: '"Tristan" in the Composition of "Pelléas"', *19CM*, v (1981–2), 117–41

A. Csampai and D. Holland, eds.: *Rororo Opernbücher: Tristan und Isolde* (Reinbek bei Hamburg, 1982)

W. Kinderman: 'Das Geheimnis der Form in Wagners "Tristan und Isolde"', *AMw*, xl (1983), 174–88

R. Knapp: 'The Tonal Structure of *Tristan und Isolde*: a Sketch', *MR*, xlv (1984), 11–25

R. Bailey, ed.: *Richard Wagner: Prelude and Transfiguration from 'Tristan and Isolde'* (New York, 1985) [Norton Critical Score]

W. Ashbrook: 'The First Singers of *Tristan und Isolde*', *OQ*, iii/4 (1985–6), 11–23

A. Groos: 'Appropriation in Wagner's *Tristan* Libretto', *Reading Opera*, ed. A. Groos and R. Parker (Princeton, NJ, 1988), 12–33

Die Meistersinger von Nürnberg

J. Tiersot: *Etude sur les Maîtres-chanteurs de Nuremberg de Richard Wagner* (Paris, 1899)

R. Sternfeld: 'Hans Sachsens Schusterlied', *Die Musik*, i (1901–2), 1869–75

K. Grunsky: 'Reim und musikalische Form in den Meistersingern', *Richard Wagner-Jb*, v (1913), 138–87

O. Strobel: '"Morgenlich leuchtend in rosigem Schein": wie Walthers "Preislied" entstand', *Bayreuther Festspielführer 1933*, 148–60

R.W. Stock: *Richard Wagner und die Stadt der Meistersinger* (Nuremberg and Berlin, 1938)

R.M. Rayner: *Wagner and 'Die Meistersinger'* (London, 1940)

W.E. Mcdonald: 'Words, Music, and Dramatic Development in "Die Meistersinger"', *19CM*, i (1977–8), 246–60

R. Brinkmann: 'Über das Kern- und Schlusswort der "Meistersinger"', *Bayerische Staatsoper: Meistersinger Programmheft zur Neuinszenierung* (Munich, 1979), 82–91

E. Voss: 'Gedanken über "Meistersinger"-Dokumente', *Bayerische Staatsoper: Meistersinger Programmheft zur Neuinszenierung* (Munich, 1979), 76–81

A. Csampai and D. Holland, eds.: *Rororo Opernbücher: Die Meistersinger von Nürnberg* (Reinbek bei Hamburg, 1981) [incl. E. Voss: 'Wagners "Meistersinger" als Oper des deutschen Bürgertums', 9–31; Eng. trans., *Wagner*, xi (1990), 39–62]

R. Turner: '"Die Meistersinger von Nürnberg": the Conceptual Growth of an Opera', *Wagner*, iii (1982), 2–16

J. Wildgruber: 'Das Geheimnis der "Barform" in R. Wagners *Die Meistersinger von Nürnberg*: Plädoyer für eine neue Art der Formbetrachtung', *Festschrift Heinz Becker*, ed. J. Schläder and R. Quandt (Laaber, 1982), 205–13

N. John, ed.: *The Mastersingers of Nuremberg* (London, 1983) [ENO opera guide]

E. Voss: 'Die Entstehung der Meistersinger von Nürnberg: Geschichten und Geschichte' (Mainz, 1983), 7–19 [facs. edn of 1862 lib.]

L'avant-scène opéra, nos.116–17 (1989) [*Die Meistersinger* issue]

B. Millington: 'Nuremberg Trial: is there Anti-Semitism in *Die Meistersinger?*', *COJ*, iii (1991), 247–60

S. Spencer: 'Wagner's Nuremberg', *COJ*, iv (1992), 21–41

A. Groos: 'Constructing Nuremberg: Typological and Proleptic Communities in *Die Meistersinger*', *19CM*, xvi (1992–3), 18–34

J. Warrack, ed.: *Richard Wagner: 'Die Meistersinger von Nürnberg'* (Cambridge, 1994)

Parsifal

H. von Wolzogen: *Thematischer Leitfaden durch die Musik zu R. Wagner's Parsifal* (Leipzig, 1882; Eng. trans., 1889)

A. Lorenz: 'Parsifal als Übermensch', *Die Musik*, i (1901–2), 1876–82

K. Grunsky: 'Die Rhythmik im Parsifal', *Richard Wagner-Jb*, iii (1908), 276–370

H. von Wolzogen: 'Parsifal-Varianten: eine Übersicht', *Richard Wagner-Jb*, iv (1912), 168–83

W. Golther: *Parsifal und der Gral in deutscher Sage des Mittelalters und der Neuzeit* (Leipzig, 1913)

C. Debussy: 'Richard Wagner', *Monsieur Croche, antidilettante* (Paris, 1921, 2/1926; Eng. trans., 1927/R), chap.16

V. d'Indy: *Introduction à l'étude de 'Parsifal'* (Paris, 1937)

T.W. Adorno: 'Zur Partitur des "Parsifal": neu gedrückte Aufsätze 1928 bis 1962', *Moments musicaux* (Frankfurt, 1964), 52–7

M. Geck and E. Voss, eds.: *Dokumente zur Entstehung und ersten Aufführung des Bühnenweihfestspiels Parsifal, Richard Wagner: Sämtliche Werke*, xxx (Mainz, 1970)

W. Keller: 'Von Meyerbeers "Robert der Teufel" zum zweiten Aufzug "Parsifal"', *Tribschener Blätter*, xxx (1971), 6–12; Eng. trans., *Wagner*, xiii (1992), 83–90

H.-J. Bauer: *Wagners Parsifal: Kriterien der Kompositionstechnik* (Munich, 1977)

P. Wapnewski: 'Parzifal und Parsifal oder Wolframs Held und Wagners Erlöser', *Richard Wagner: von der Oper zum Musikdrama*, ed. S. Kunze (Berne and Munich, 1978), 47–60

J. Chailley: *'Parsifal' de Richard Wagner: opéra initiatique* (Paris, 1979)

L. Beckett: *Richard Wagner: Parsifal* (Cambridge, 1981)

L'avant-scène opéra, nos.38–9 (1982) [*Parsifal* issue]

A. Csampai and D. Holland, eds.: *Rororo Opernbücher: Parsifal* (Reinbek bei Hamburg, 1982)

H.-K. Metzger and R. Riehn, eds.: *Richard Wagner: Parsifal*, Musik-Konzepte, no.25 (Munich, 1982)

W. Seelig: 'Ambivalenz und Erlösung – Wagners "Parsifal": Zweifel und Glauben', *ÖMz*, xxxvii (1982), 307–17

B. Millington: 'Parsifal: Facing the Contradictions', *MT*, cxxiv (1983), 97–8

D. Lewin: 'Amfortas's Prayer to Titurel and the Role of D in *Parsifal*', *19CM*, vii (1983–4), 336–49

N. John, ed.: *Parsifal* (London, 1986) [ENO opera guide]

M.A. Cicora: *'Parsifal' Reception in the 'Bayreuther Blätter'* (Frankfurt, Berne and New York, 1987)

B. Millington: '"Parsifal": a Wound Reopened', *Wagner*, viii (1987), 114–20

M. Geck: 'Parsifal: a Betrayed Childhood', *Wagner*, ix (1988), 75–88

B. Millington: '"Parsifal": a Work for our Times', *Opera*, xxxix (1988), 13–17

B. Emslie: 'Woman as Image and Narrative in Wagner's *Parsifal*: a Case Study', *COJ*, iii (1991), 109–24

Other works

W. Kleefeld: 'Richard Wagner als Bearbeiter fremder Werke', *Die Musik*, iv/2 (1904–5), 231–49, 326–37

K. Mey: 'Über Richard Wagners Huldigungschor an König Friedrich August II. von Sachsen 1844', *Die Musik*, v/1 (1905–6), 327–31

K. Mey: 'Richard Wagners Webertrauermarsch', *Die Musik*, vi/2 (1906–7), 331–6

E. Istel: 'Eine Doppelfuge von der Hand Wagners: nach dem ungedruckten Original-manuskript mitgeteilt', *Die Musik*, xi/4 (1911–12), 27–41

E. Istel: 'Ein unbekanntes Instrumentalwerk Wagners: auf Grund der handschriftlichen Partitur dargestellt', *Die Musik*, xii/3 (1912–13), 152–7

H.W. von Waltershausen: *Das Siegfried-Idyll, oder die Rückkehr zur Natur* (Munich, 1920)

R. Sternfeld: 'Die erste Fassung von Wagners Faust-Ouvertüre', *Die Musik*, xv (1922–3), 659–64

O. Strobel: 'Das "Porazzi"-Thema: über eine unveröffentlichte Melodie Richard Wagners und deren seltsamer Werdegang', *Bayreuther Festspielführer 1934*, 183

G. Abraham: 'Wagner's String Quartet: an Essay in Musical Speculation', *MT*, lxxxvi (1945), 233–4

W.S. Newman: 'Wagner's Sonatas', *Studies in Romanticism*, vii (1968), 129

E. Voss: 'Wagners fragmentarisches Orchesterwerk in e-moll: die früheste der erhaltenen Kompositionen?', *Mf*, xxiii (1970), 50–54

B. Millington: 'Wagner's Works for Piano', *Wagner 1976: a Celebration of the Bayreuth Festival*, ed. S. Spencer (London, 1976), 30–38

E. Voss: *Richard Wagner und die Instrumentalmusik: Wagners symphonischer Ehrgeiz* (Wilhelmshaven, 1977)

J. Deathridge: 'Richard Wagners Kompositionen zu Goethes "Faust"', *Jb der Bayerischen Staatsoper* (Munich, 1982), 90

E. Voss: *Richard Wagner: eine Faust-Ouvertüre* (Munich, 1982)

I. Vetter, ed.: '"Leubald: ein Trauerspiel": Richard Wagners erstes (erhaltenes) Werk', *Bayreuther Festspiele: Programmheft VII. Die Meistersinger* (Bayreuth, 1998), 1–19, 95–208 [incl. Eng. trans., and transcr. of complete text]

S. Spencer, ed.: '"Die hohe Braut": an Unpublished Draft', *Wagner*, x (1989), 50–65

O: Wagnerism

O.W. Peterson-Berger: *Richard Wagner als Kulturscheinung* (Leipzig, 1917)

K. Hildebrandt: *Wagner und Nietzsche: ihr Kampf gegen das 19. Jahrhundert* (Breslau, 1924)

J. Barzun: *Darwin, Marx, Wagner: Critique of a Heritage* (Boston, 1941, 2/1958)

E. Bentley: 'Wagner and Ibsen: a Contrast', *The Modern Theatre: a Study of Dramatists and the Drama* (London, 1948), 64–90

T.W. Adorno: *Versuch über Wagner* (Berlin and Frankfurt, 1952; Eng. trans., as *In Search of Wagner*, 1981)

H. Kirchmeyer: *Das zeitgenössische Wagner-Bild*, i–vii (Regensburg, 1967–)

B. Magee: *Aspects of Wagner* (London, 1968, 3/1988)

A. Ziino, ed.: *Antologia della critica wagneriana in Italia* (Messina, 1970)

S. Grossmann-Vendrey: *Bayreuth in der deutschen Presse*, ii: *Die Uraufführung des Parsifal* (Regensburg, 1977)

S. Martin: *Wagner to 'The Waste Land': a Study of the Relationship of Wagner to English Literature* (London, 1982)

Richard Wagner: Salzburg 1983

M. Kahane and N. Wild, eds.: *Wagner et la France* (Paris, 1983)

J. Kerman: 'Wagner and Wagnerism', *New York Review* (22 Dec 1983)

D.C. Large and W. Weber, eds.: *Wagnerism in European Culture and Politics* (Ithaca, NY, 1984)

J. Horowitz: *Wagner Nights: an American History* (Berkeley and Los Angeles, 1994)

A. Hein: *'Es ist viel "Hitler" in Wagner': Rassismus und antisemitische Deutschtumsideologie in den 'Bayreuther Blättern' (1878–1938)* (Tübingen, 1996)

A. Schneider: *Die parodierten Musikdramen Richard Wagners* (Anif, Salzburg, 1996)

J. Köhler: *Wagners Hitler: Der Prophet und sein Vollstrecker* (Munich, 1997)

INDEX